THE

FORGOTTEN

ISRAELITES

GOD'S CHOSEN PEOPLE

Another Bible Companion

Written By Shadrock

THIS IS SOMETHING THAT HAD TO BE DONE
A MESSAGE THAT I HAD TO DELIVER TO A PEOPLE
WHOSE LIVES ARE DETERIORATING AND BECOMING
MORE AND MORE CRITICAL WITH EVERY PASSING DAY
Shadrock...

FOR MORE INFORMATION

ON THIS

VERY IMPORTANT SUBJECT

CONCERNING THE CHILDREN OF SLAVERY

THE FORGOTTEN ISRAELITES

You must also
READ
THE TRUTH THE LIE AND THE BIBLE
By Shadrock

FIRST EDITION
No part of this book may be used, copied, printed or broadcast in whole or in part
without the consent in writing from the Publishers.
This book was edited by : Mr. Michael Hinds
Cover is designed by the author : Shadrock
All Rights Reserved
Copyright © 1991
by
FIFTH RIBB PUBLISHING
P.O. Box 287 Station E.
Toronto Ontario M6H-4E2
Canada

ISBN 0-9694907-1-2
Printed in Canada

THIS BOOK IS DEDICATED
TO ALL WOMEN
Especially my mother
Estelle (Baby) Muss
A strong woman of colour
Who died in 1981
To all women like her
Who are now fortunate to be alive
And have the opportunity to choose between
Right and wrong

THE FORGOTTEN ISRAELITES
God's Chosen People

INDEX   PAGE

1 Preface... 7

2 Introduction.. 11

3 Don't Call Me Brother................................. 19
   The West-Indian Connection 29
   Edom and Israel, Islam and Christianity.................... 39
   The Birth of Edom and Israel........................ 46

4 All You Need To Know About Saints.............. 55
   The Invisible Being.................................... 63

5 W.O.M.A.N.. 76
   Blackwomen in Leadership 78
   The Spiritual Aspect................................. 81
   Feminine Influence & Strength.................... 83
   The Era of Witches 88
   Women Misunderstood.............................. 91
   Circumcision & Your Baby 93
   Marriage and You.................................... 98
   The Unwed Mother..................................107
   Her Weakness 109
   The Fountain 111

6 To Be An Israelite....................................117
   The Textbook..117
   Your Apparel 118
   Incense 120
   Use Water not Wine 120
   The Cross...122
   How to Worship 123
   God's Day 125
   The Truth about Fire & Hell......................125
   The Real Colours of the Blackman 128
   Your Eating Habits...................................130

7 Stand Before The Mirror...........................134

PREFACE

First I would like to thank my God, the God of my fathers, who is the God of Abraham, the God of Isaac, and the God of Israel, for giving me the greatest gift of all, Life. I also would like to thank Him for leading me through the passageway of ignorance and darkness, into the hallway of brightness and wisdom, and for bestowing upon me the power of understanding which are the gifts of the Prophets.

I thank the family that I was blessed with, for their patience and encouragement, their undivided support and attention. Thanks to Michael for taking the time so precious to him, to edit this book. To Tony and the council members of Israel for being there. I cannot allow the space to be taken up without giving special thanks to Laney. There is not enough space to express my gratitude. To do so now, would not be fair to you my readers, but without her patience and understanding, this project would have taken a little longer.

I thank God for the race of people for which I belong, for without them, the zeal to fight might not have been there. There would have been no need for food, if there was no hunger, or the need for clothes if there was no nakedness. There would not have been the need to fight, if there were no enemies, or the need to teach if there was no ignorance. If there were no children then there would have been no Prophets. If there were no fathers, there would have been no children. If there was no God, there would have been no FORGOTTEN ISRAELITES.

In the early 70's there was a stream of black Americans flowing into Africa and the Caribbean, especially Guyana, looking for ways to rid themselves of the burdens they faced at home in the U.S.A., and at the same time assisted those countries with their skills, in whatever way they could. One such person was Tom Feeling. I met Tom when he was in Guyana. He was working for the Ministry of Information and Culture at that time. He was an illustrator, and I was a supervisor. One day Tom came into my office and forgot his book on my desk. The book was called "One Hundred Amazing Facts About The American Negro" by J.A. Rogers. Tom never saw that book again, I took it. This book brought back so many memories of my grandfather's teaching, that I promised myself never to relax until I fulfilled the dreams of this great man of colour.

Knowing the history of my people grabbed me then, but soon after I realized that such knowledge was not good enough, if you cannot put it to work for the benefit of the present day situation. So after years of research, I've decided to teach my people much more than their history, but Christianity was, and still is, the greatest threat just like the bible predicted in Revelation, but that will never stop me. That is why I am thankful for my teachers, the God of Israel and my earthly grandfather. Anyhow, wherever you are Tom, I thank you and sincerely hope that I will be able to see you again and return your book. May the God of my fathers bless you real good.

I have always said that teaching the doctrine of truth was not going to be easy. I am sure you know by now that I was right. Those of you who have read THE TRUTH THE LIE AND THE BIBLE and started to teach from it, know what I'm saying is true.

Those of you who have been calling me from all over North America to thank me, allow me to use this opportunity to thank you. To those of you who are with me, you have had your days of glory. You have listened to the ignorant calling you names, but never ever able to prove you wrong. Don't worry, just go on and be proud for the truth is not for every man's heart; just the chosen of God.

Jeremiah 31:33 "But this shall be the COVENANT that I will make with the HOUSE OF ISRAEL; After those days, saith the Lord, I will put my law in their INWARD PARTS, and **write it in their hearts**; and will be their God, and they shall be my people."

This book was also written for my brethren, because of the overflow of love between us and our God. We give God thanks this day for the knowledge and power that He has bestowed on us.

You have watched the ones who could not understand. They have provided you with the opportunity to have the last laugh. I say now the time for you to laugh at them is over. Teach them about your power. You should always remember that it was this truth that made them kill Jesus. John 18:37 "Pilate therefore said unto him, Art thou a king then? Jesus answered, Thou sayest that I am a king. To this end was I born, and for this cause came I into the world, that I should bear witness unto the TRUTH. Every one that is of the truth heareth my voice."

The truth will always be the enemy of the lie, so if you find that the disciples of Lucifer hate you. Rejoice! For you have found

8

a greater love. The prophets had died because of truth, that you may live in that truth, and see that truth. For fools cannot see even with their own eyes, neither can they hear with their own ears.

Romans 11:8 "(According as it is written, God hath given them the SPIRIT OF SLUMBER, eyes that they should not see, and ears that they should not hear;) unto this day."

We who are practising Israelites, who do the will of our God are fortunate to have this truth. Knowing quite well that there are Israelites out there in this world that are caught up in false doctrine and remain sincere to that lie because of ignorance. To them I say enlarge your heart and do not be like some of your fathers of old. SEEK THE TRUTH.

John 8:44-45 "Ye are of your father the devil, and the lusts of your father ye will do. He was a murderer from the beginning, and abode not in the TRUTH, because there is no TRUTH in him. When he speaketh a lie, he speaketh of his own: for he is a liar, and the father of it.
AND BECAUSE I TELL YOU THE TRUTH, YE BELIEVE ME NOT."

Isaiah 56:8-11 "The Lord God which gathereth the outcasts of Israel saith, Yet will I gather others to him, beside those that are gathered unto him.
All ye beasts of the field, come to devour, yea, all ye beasts in the forest.
His watchmen are BLIND: they are all IGNORANT, they are all DUMB DOGS, they cannot bark; sleeping, lying down, loving to slumber.
Yea, they are greedy dogs which can never have enough, and they are shepherds that cannot understand: they all look to their own way, every one for his gain, from his quarter."

I personally cannot describe in words the power of His Spirit who is my teacher, who has given me knowledge, beyond those who lead in our society, beyond those whose influence is great in our society, beyond those who are my unknown enemies, beyond the teachers of Christianity.

HEAR OH ISRAEL THE LORD OUR GOD, THE LORD IS ONE! Let me say thanks to all of you for believing in one God, the only Almighty God, the God of my Fathers, The God of Abraham, The God of Isaac, and the God of Jacob, The True and Living God of Israel. There is none other under heaven and upon this earth that is mightier than He. Let His name be praised from everlasting to everlasting. Thank you again my brethren, and I hope that others who still have the spirit of slumber will see that light shining on you and one day will understand and believe in the GOD OF ALL SPIRITS, MY FATHER.

INTRODUCTION

Before we enter into the light of knowledge, before we turn the pages of wisdom, let us try to understand the meaning of our being. Let us try to understand life. Let us divide life with the hatchet of understanding and examine both sides, for only then can we understand the truth from the lie. Only then will we be able to gain spiritual strength over physical weaknesses. We will be able to turn our rags of doom into clothing of light.

Stand up weak one. Get up on your feet. Throw away the clothing of Christianity and STAND TALL, DARK AND SMART. Do not allow anyone to tell you lies that will affect you for the rest of your life. Christians say if you're not a Jew, then you're a Gentile - LIE - Moses was not a Jew. Exodus 2:1-10. Paul was not a Jew. READ Romans 11:1 "I say then, Hath God cast away his people? God forbid. **For I also am an Israelite**, of the seed of Abraham, of the tribe of Benjamin."

Others say all black people are Muslims - LIE - Jesus was not a Muslim. He was an Israelite from the seed of Judah, a Jew. Matthew 2:2 "Saying, Where is he that is born KING OF THE JEWS? for we have seen his star in the east, and are come to worship him." Abraham was not a Muslim. Isaac was not a Muslim. Jacob was not a Muslim. They served the God of Israel.

Exodus 3:15 "And God said moreover unto Moses, Thus shalt thou say unto the children of Israel, The Lord God of your fathers, The God of Abraham, the God of Isaac, and the God of Jacob, hath sent me unto you THIS IS MY NAME FOR EVER, and this is my memorial unto all generations."

The misconception that you believed all along that these prophets were white Anglo Saxon is not true. It is the biggest lie ever told to keep black people in mental slavery.

Some black people are suddenly becoming like the Edomites, insisting that you learn Hebrew. What Hebrew? What language did Moses speak, when he spoke to God on the mount? What language could a cultured Egyptian prince speak? He spoke Egyptian. Do you know any African language? No! Because you've been here in the Americas for almost 400 years, similar to the 430 years the Israelites spent in Egypt. Did they know Hebrew? No! They did not.

The children of Israel of today are all lost. What is important now, is to find your way back to your God and COMMUNICATE

11

with Him in any language. He gave our fathers all languages at the Tower of Babel. Therefore He knows all languages.

Genesis 11:6-9 "And the Lord said, Behold, the people is one, and they have all one language; and this they begin to do: and now nothing will be restrained from them, which they have imagined to do.

Go to, let us go down and there confound their language, that they may not understand one another's speech.

So the Lord scattered them abroad from thence upon the face of all the earth: and they left off to build the city.

Therefore is the name of it called Babel; because THE LORD DID THERE CONFOUND THE LANGUAGE OF ALL THE EARTH: and from thence did the Lord scatter them abroad upon the face of all the earth."

It was all languages that were being spoken on the day of Pentecost. Acts 2:6 "Now when this was noised abroad, the multitude came together, and were confounded, because that every man heard them speak in his own language."

The Hebrew nation started with our father Abraham, it was not in existence when he was first called by the name Abram, if this was so, then Ishmael would have been a Hebrew. So when the Israelites began leaving the land of Israel, their language and customs slowly began to deteriorate. It was noted, around the third century B.C that the language being used then in Palestine, (Old Israel) was not the real Hebrew that was spoken by our fathers before, instead they were speaking ARAMAIC, which is also a Semitic language, closely related to Hebrew. It was a real mystery at that time, and still is, but because of the flow of other dialects and customs, which came about through the many battles, and the domination by foreign powers, the language situation was taken for granted. The few Jews that remained in the land, began researching, and came up with what they called then the MISHNAH. The Mishnaic Hebrew was strongly influenced by Greek and Latin. In the 11th to the 14th century the Mishnaic Hebrew was again revised, this time with a strong Arabic influence. Today's Hebrew has a strong European flavour, for the people that now use it, are originally from Europe. So what is all this talk about Hebrew?

The original Hebrew language was used by our fathers to praise God. Now our real God is lost, and so is our real language. In the same way the scriptures state that we would not see the land anymore, it's the same way we can't speak that language anymore, and there is nothing any man can do about it. Our only hope is through KNOWLEDGE, WISDOM, AND UNDERSTANDING. Do not be caught up in the language issue, which is physical, and miss the most important aspect in life. YOUR SPIRITUALITY.

Remember two things 1) You are not a Christian. You are an Israelite. Plus, it would make perfect sense if you serve the God of Israel, for He is the only God written about in the Holy Bible that the Christians use. Why pretend that you pray to one God while you read about another. Isn't that a hypocritical behaviour?
2) You are not a Muslim. It was the Muslims who sold our fathers to Christians for slaves. Even if this does not convince you, think about this: it was the Egyptians that were God's enemy who enslaved our fathers, the Israelites.

Why would you want to be on the side of the enemy of God and still say you love Him? It is alright to know the history of Egypt and the Pyramids, but what good would it do if you're still in jail, still with diseases and sickness, still in poverty and despair. Some of our fathers had no choice but to fight as Muslims because it was the prophecy that Ishmael would dwell with his brethren, but that time has past. Zion is crying again for her children.

When your 400 years are up what are you going to be? Still stupid, still blind, still in poverty? Wake up Israel! Our God is alive. Come on home you Forgotten Israelites. If God is my judge then whom shall I fear?

I remember in 1981 I was visiting my friend Kessel, who lived in the vicinity of Jane Street and Finch Avenue West. It was during the winter of that year and very cold. Since I don't drive I decided to take the public transit. I don't know how, but I ended up on Eglinton Avenue West. That day I thought I was fortunate, as I looked towards the bus shelter there was a lone occupant already there. It must have been a Sunday, because the woman in the shelter was showing off her apparel that fitted snugly around her black skin, hat and all. I couldn't help but to be polite, and even though my teeth were clutched together and my ears left me because of the cold, I still found breath to say hello. She replied very nicely, she even gave me a bonus smile. I said to myself this must be my lucky day. She smiled again. I smiled back, and got up enough courage to ask her a very stupid question.

"Where are you heading?" I asked. "To church," she replied. Stupid me I said under my breath. I should have known. When a black woman dresses like this, bible under her arm, packing a smile a mile long, even talking to you, it has to be Sunday, and she must be going to church, otherwise my name is Jack.

"What were you saying?" she asked. "I thought you said something. Pardon me!"

She had perfect teeth too. I was trying to play my little game that I use to play in those days. By looking at a black person, I would try to determine which tribe or house they're from. I imagined in my mind that she had to be Jewish. For Jews are elegantly blessed with perfect teeth and brown eyes almost red and she fitted the picture. So I asked knowing that her answer would be a ridiculous one; I found out later her answer was far worse.

"Are you Jewish?" I asked mockingly.

"Are you crazy! I'm a Christian." She had a question of her own I found out when she asked me. "Say, you found Jesus yet?" Again those teeth revealed themselves as her lips parted into the smile I learnt to appreciate in our brief meeting.

"Is He lost? Am I suppose to find Him?" Now there were no teeth, no smile and no jokes. "Do you go to church? She asked. "Have you accepted Jesus in your life?" I began to laugh.

"What's so funny?" She said. "Don't you know that Jesus died for our sins? Don't you know that if you believe in Him you'll have everlasting life?" I laughed again.

Then she took out her bible and right there on the inside page was the white man with long blonde hair and a lot of little thorns coming out of his head.

She was getting ready now to preach, to hold down her one-man audience, using the bus shelter for her church. "You must be born again, Jesus loves you. You must be born again." she insisted.

I was beginning to believe that this woman was waiting for me to come into this shelter, just so she could spank me with her philosophy. So very politely I asked her name. She refused, so I called her Miss. I said, "Miss, Are you born again?"

Her reply along with all the dramatic trimmings was, "Of course, I found my Saviour. Now I know my Saviour."

Then I asked her since she knew Him so well, if she wouldn't mind telling me what He looked like.

She reached for her bible again. Her forefinger tapped on the nose of the picture in her bible.

"My Jesus, My Lord." she replied. So I told her, "If that

14

picture or that man in the picture is your Lord, you are doomed. If you can show me anywhere in your bible where your picture fits the recorded description I'll come to your church right now."

I asked her, "Miss, how can you be born again and be a Christian? If you are indeed born again then you are suppose to be of truth. Can you tell me as a Christian anything that you do, any instruction that you follow that is written in the bible, apart from John 3:16?"

"We love, brother. We Love," she replied. I then told her that she had no need for the bible, just love sister, love.

By this time our bus arrived, she looked down the streets at the approaching bus, then looked at me, and delivered a mouthful of saliva that I'm sure must have damaged the sidewalk. I suddenly realized that she was too decent to spit on me, so she imagined that I looked like the side walk, and she let me have it right between the eyes.

A beautiful Forgotten Israelite who just called me brother, generated enough hate to last her for a long time through simple and truthful questions. She is gone and I'm sure is proud to be walking in the dark. There are millions of Forgotten Israelites who are not aware of themselves.

I met Madge who called herself a mother of a small church. She asked me one day to visit her church on Lansdowne Avenue. At first I thought it was against my policy to worship on Sunday, but she made it appear as though I would have the opportunity to teach. So I seized the opportunity to do God's work.

When I first entered the small church, the spirit left my body. I could not sing along with them, I could not be at one with them no matter how I tried. So I prayed and prayed silently. Suddenly out of nowhere, there was a dog barking in the distance and the sound began to draw nearer and nearer. Then I remembered what the Spirit had taught me, that the sound or likeness of a dog is evil. My mind raced to Ecclesiastes 3:21 "Who knoweth the spirit of man that goeth upward, and the spirit of the beast that goeth downward to the earth?"

After careful thought I realized that I was in the wrong place, then I thought maybe the spirit of God must have placed me for a direct confrontation with this evil. Again my mind turned the pages of the scriptures, and I felt sorry for these people displaying all this ignorance. Later on this woman was proudly proclaiming her gift of the spirits. I wondered if she ever took the time to read

15

Revelation 22:14-15 "Blessed are they that do his commandments, that they may have right to the tree of life, and may enter in through the gates into the city.
FOR WITHOUT ARE DOGS, and sorcerers, and whoremongers, and murderers, and idolaters, AND WHOSOEVER LOVETH AND MAKETH A LIE."

I looked down from my prayer and the woman in the chair in front of me was really barking like a dog. I began to sweat, my feet lifted from off the ground. I heard Madge calling out to me, so I moved to the front of the church. When I felt the presence of the Spirit I realized I was to shut up and let God's will be done. The voice within me told Madge to take all her images down and to turn the place into a House of God, for the God of Israel.

The place was quiet, so the sound of the disapproval of the dog seemed to be getting louder through the body of this woman. The next Sunday I was not invited, but I went anyway. I stayed at the back of the church while everyone was reading scriptures as directed by Madge (mother). Also in attendance was a man whom I later found out was a leader of another small spiritual church. While he was reading the scripture that he had chosen, he stopped, and looked back at me. I had never seen him before in my life. He said to Madge, "I think this brother has a lot to say." Madge suddenly stood up at her pulpit and screamed at me. "No! No! When he speaks I can't eat. I can't sleep. No! No! Don't let him speak."

In the sea of my embarrassment I managed to hold my head high, just waiting for the end. Afterwards nobody shook my hand or waved, so I waved, said goodbye and left. I never felt happier when the cool fresh air caressed my face outside the doors of that little church. In the three weeks that I came to know Madge and her husband, I had replaced a shabby twisted sign in front of the church with a perfectly professionally painted one. However, as I was passing Madge's church on my way to the subway the following Monday morning, the perfectly good sign that I had donated was replaced with the old shabby one. Their little church lasted a couple of weeks after that, then they were gone, but it did not close the chapter of mother Madge. I hope she is still not confused, still wants to serve God, but still not in the wilderness of ignorance. For such is the way of the faithful Christian.

I would not tell you the story about the newspaper in Toronto that refused to review "The Truth The Lie and The Bible." Why

16

tell it, for they too are no longer. The editor pleaded with me not to say anything bad about Christianity, and after she discovered on which side I stood on the subject, she refused to have anything to do with me. This woman was willing to die for the cause of Christianity, both man and church.

For all these people God has taken second and third place in their lives. Their church, its philosophy and their pastor are far more important than God. I hope one day that black people in the Americas will learn about their true identity and turn away from the evils of the lie. The great deception of the Christian church and the seed it has planted in the hearts and minds of God's chosen people has turned them away from Him; causing them to dwell in the pits of darkness, despair, sickness and disease, spiritual ignorance and disrespect.

This book is written to provide answers to the many questions that are being asked by truth seekers. This book is written for the ones who dwell in ignorance. This book is written for black people in the Americas. To provide them with a spiritual sword of the Lord's truth. This book is written for white people who might feel everything white is right. It provides them with the knowledge of their black ancestors. Luke 5:31 "And Jesus answering said unto them, They that are whole need not a physician: but they that are SICK."

This book is sending out a challenge to all liars and traditionalists who dare to teach from the book of the Israelite without the knowledge of its content, and corrupt the minds of God's chosen people, The FORGOTTEN ISRAELITES. Beware of those biblical scholars who tell you that Abraham was a Jew, and call themselves Reverend. This is the first sign of their ignorance. Remember spiritual things can only be taught by the SPIRIT, and the things of God, taught only by His Spirit.

Only the name of God is REVEREND, not man. Psalm 111: 9 "He sent redemption unto his people: he hath commanded his covenant forever; HOLY AND REVEREND IS HIS NAME."

Do not allow yourselves to be led anymore by the blind, for the end of the four hundred years is just around the corner. Wake up my people, Return to your God, and BEWARE OF FALSE PROPHETS, AND WOLVES IN SHEEP CLOTHING.

May the light shine upon you as you turn the following pages, bearing in mind that knowledge is power. Wisdom is strength and understanding is the essence of life itself.

17

You may now put this book down and return to what you were doing and close this chapter forever in your life, or you may continue on, and the following pages will provide you with the sword of power, and a knowledge that will teach you how to use it.

Just imagine that we are in a conference room together exploring ways that will enable us to bring the children of slavery back to some measure of respectability, to make them aware of their identity, and their responsibility, to their God, their race and the world at large.

It is now my turn to say something. Just imagine I am talking to you my people What I have to say is written in THE FOLLOWING PAGES...

DON'T CALL ME BROTHER

Don't call me brother
And take the last coat that I've got
How the hell am I your brother
And you're stabbing me in the back
Don't call me brother
While you're holding a gun to my head
What kind of a brother are you
Wanting me dead
Don't call me brother
And don't give a damn about me
How can we be brothers
When you can't even recognize me
Don't call me brother
When you're way over there
We can never be brothers
Cause I'm cold and lonely down here
Don't call me brother
When you don't know my mommy
You are not my brother
You killed my Daddy
Don't call me brother
When your big boots walk on my toe
Brothers feel the pain
Of their brothers in the ghetto
Don't call me brother
When it don't mean a thing
You moved out of town
Cause you made it big
Don't call me brother
When you're making millions

A big brother would care
About the little ones
Don't call me brother
Raising your fist up high
Cause you never saw the tears
Coming from my eye
Don't call me brother
Cause you only look like me
We lost that bond
Long after slavery
Now you're calling me brother
Oh why can't you see
We are not brothers
Cause we're not a family
You have another father
And I retain our old Dad
So please don't call me brother
The whole situation is so SAD

First of all, let us look at the facts on Christianity. Who upholds it, cherishes it, kills for it and most of all judges by it? The western countries, particularly Britain and the United States. After they found that they could capitalize on it, the way Constantine of Rome did, they embraced it and went to great lengths to protect it, changing it from time to time to suit their political and economical needs. Bearing in mind that Britain reluctantly handed over world policing to the U.S. The spiritual meaning of all this, began to unfold later on. For example, the British never entertained the thought of keeping black slaves in England because, if I might add, this would not have been according to biblical prophecy. That leading power, which kept black slaves on their soil eventually would be the richest and most powerful nation in the world, at the end of the predicted four hundred years. Such a country would play the role or take the place of a second Egypt.

For this reason the United States was made the new or spiritual Egypt while black men and women (the true Israelites) were enslaved again, as prophesied in Deuteronomy. Please note carefully that the United States of America with all its might and power, never, I repeat, never attacked another white nation. They were reluctantly fighting against Hitler's Germany. They only did so because of pressure from Britain, their close ally and friend, who remained the only white Anglo Saxon race that the U.S. really fought; and the reason? Simple! INDEPENDENCE.

They got involved in the Second World War because of Pearl Harbour being bombed by the Japanese. Had it not been for Pearl Harbour, the United States would not have fired one single shot at white Germany. The same goes for the First World War. The United States must have felt terrible after the rest of the western world was in fierce battle with Germany after the invasion of Serbia (Yugoslavia) in 1914. It was not until 1917 before the United States again reluctantly entered the war which ended in the next year 1918. Please note that against non-white nations the United States is always in the lead to fight and destroy, while with a white nation she is always the last to enter the conflict.

This is also a reflection of her domestic policy. The rights of the Blackman are always covered with the coat of discrimination and prejudice. To put it bluntly there are no rights other than on paper. That paper is used for the convenience of the system, to call on the records in a court of law. The Blackman continues to hang on to that paper and to hope for legislation that cannot, and will never set him free. Just like the way it was in old Egypt when the children of Israel waited for their Deliverer. Today, that Deliverer remains the same. THE GOD OF ISRAEL.

The white god can't help the Blackman of the Americas, neither can the imitators of false doctrine. There is much need for the Blackman to know who he is. **History alone can only play a part, but it is not the solution.**

Until the Blackman of the Americas realizes that he is not a Muslim nor a Christian, the better would his life be. The sooner he realises that he is the true Israelite, descendent of Jacob (Israel), the sooner he returns to his God, the more successful and progressive he will be.

Everywhere the American, British and others of their sort went they preached without the spirit, about the spirit. You who have the spirit, put it away for emptiness, like the dog and the bone.

21

(The dog was travelling on a bridge over the lake with a perfectly good and eatable bone. The reflection of his own bone enlarged in the stream caused him to drop the real one for the reflection. He ended up without.) The Blackman has given up his way of life and his greatness for jail, dope, prostitution, sickness and disease.

When he looks in the mirror of life all he sees is his own ugliness and the beauty of others, that beauty he carries with him from day to day. What is worse is the philosophy of others and their gods. Again, he sees the beauty of their god and cannot see his own. Even the ugliness of his own God would be scary and perhaps, someday, this would reflect in his mind.So he has decided to erase him and make him none existence.

The same way he had thrown away his God, his God had thrown him away. The only way back for him is through the God of his fathers. The God of Israel. He cannot retain his full dignity through political or physical means. A spiritual solution is the Blackman's only hope.

The same way the Christians have taken the spirits from the Indians and left them in the wilderness of destruction and despair, in like manner have they taken the Blackman's God away from him. The only difference is, the Indians know and realize their calamity, but the Blackman continues to seek political and physical solutions while still holding on to the god of his enemy.

With all the Blackmen in Congress, all the black mayors, all the millions circulating to and from black hands, they still have no control. They no longer ride the back of the bus, they now own the bus, so why are they still in lamentation? Why do they still mourn for their sons and daughters? Why are their babies bringing home babies? Why are they still homeless? Why are one quarter of young Blackmen in jail? Why do they kill others that look like them and for what? A belt, a ghetto blaster, a watch, a pumped up sneaker, brand named trousers? Their pride is in the dust of which they are all scum, and this is how they are being seen in the eyes of the white man.

Listen to yourself and your black educators, your teachers and your preachers, who are still squeezing the last buck out of the little you have. Just listen to them. It is the economic situation placed on us by the white man.What economic situation? You are politicians now remember! Just count on your two hands and your toes how many black Congressmen there are, how many black mayors! You even have a potential, or should I say potential candidates for President. You can even vote. You were leading the army in the Gulf war. What more do you want? You can now sue the K.K.K. and win. You're in the media business, the entertainment business, the sports business and big business. You own your own colleges, universities and other places of learning, but you still have a store room full of excuses! Do you know why? Because you are in the habit of kissing the hands that whipped you. How come you are still at the bottom? Oh I forgot! It is the economic system. You are so blinded by the light of confusion that you cannot see that everything you possess adds up to nought. Including in all those things is the white man's god that you are willing to die for, while the white man is willing to kill you.

The new Egypt has given you everything that the old Egypt gave our fathers. Remember, Egypt was at it's all time high in the days of Ramses and it was in those days that the children of Israel were slaves in Egypt. Look around you today. Which is that mighty nation? Then look in your mirror and there you'll find the Israelite made a slave again.

Let's put on our abstract mind and walk in the hall of supreme art, and look at the lines, the texture of velvet smoothness, the curves that marvels nature itself and the colour that make others go to great lengths to have. The hair that is unwanted by the art itself, but rest in the vision of others.

When you stand back and look at the Forgotten Israelites who are African Americans you can't help but wonder why all the confusion. Just stand back and watch them, made up of flesh and bones that have been placed together by Supremacy, for supremacy. One must come to the conclusion that there are many reasons for others to grudge, envy, or seek to destroy.

That is why this new Egypt (U.S.A.) has been planning from the day the Israelites went into captivity again in the 17th century, to destroy them physically and spiritually. Today they are at a point of celebration - a point of victory. While the Israelites continue to have an abstract mind, but only seeing the beauty of others and their culture and most dangerous of all, seeing the beauty of strange and false gods.

No wonder when you look at television and you see and hear people like Professor Rushton speaking of how dumb black people are, you feel like strangling him with your bare hands and kicking him when he is down, but then again, that would cost you a new T.V. set.

If Professor Rushton was indeed serious about carrying out an honest research, he would have gone back to the beginning of man, trace his journeys and culture, his philosophy and his identity and I am sure that Professor Rushton would discover the ingenuity of the Blackman. For it was the Blackman that was first in the theory of evolution, and in the teachings of creation. Professor Rushton would have discovered that all cultures and civilization that were erected in this modern society were built on the foundation of this first man, but then again I am sure that this would not have been what Professor Rushton wanted to know. What he wants to know is what he has published.

Here is an example of the philosophy of Professor Rushton and the Pioneer Fund. **PIONEER FUND INC.** Tax Exempt Foundation, New York City. President: Harry F. Weyher. Established in 1937.

Original Goals: To provide aid for the study of race betterment and research of heredity and eugenics. **Eugenics** - Doubleday Dictionary - The science and art of improving a race or breed by mating individuals with desired characteristics. Many sterilization laws, as a result of eugenics, have been repealed and the Pioneer Fund has modified its charter. **BUT eugenics still remains in place.**

Opposing opinions state that the Pioneer Fund solely continues to support racial controversial research, providing grants for professors to study race, with the primary focus for decades being to show that African American peoples are intellectually inferior.

A Controversial Recipient is Dr. Philip Rushton Professor at the University of Western Ontario Canada

He has received $200,000 from funds for his research, although he states that his research is not in the field of eugenics. He claims after years of research that there are differences between the races and ranks them in categories of:

Intelligence - Criminal behaviour - Sexuality

He concludes that the Asian is the most intelligent, then the Caucasian and finally the Blackman. One of the standards he uses is head size. He has alleged that the Asian man has the largest head, therefore the largest brain and in many cases implying a slightly higher intelligence. He also states that black people have the smallest brains and the largest genitals.

He has conducted his research from books such as "Kensey

Data" where peoples have self reported the size of their penis, further showing a difference in the races.

HIS OPPONENT is Dr. Neil Weiner of York University in Canada. Dr. Weiner is writing a critique on Rushton's work, calling it RACE SCIENCE - JUNK SCIENCE. He states that much of Rushton's research data is outdated, useless and even fictional. For example: Rushton has quoted from a book titled "Untrodden Fields of Anthropology" written by a French army surgeon. This book is a century old and Weiner states that no serious professor would use this kind of material for research. This is something you might find on the cover of The National Inquirer. Dr. Weiner claims that he refuses to be associated with the Pioneer Fund or with any of its associates.

Another Recipient is Dr. William Shockley. Nobel Prize Winner in Physics - 1956. He supported...

The Voluntary Sterilization Bonus Plan
Conclusion from the Opposition
Old eugenic movements brought death camps, breeding farms and sterilization laws. What shall we expect from the new eugenics?

After reading this report I have no one to blame but the African Americans, for they are the ones who allowed and turned this garbage into gold. If they had stayed with their God and not worshipped the god of the Gentiles all this trash would not have been falling on their heads.

The Pioneer Fund to my mind was set up to walk on the Blackman. They provide the shoes for the feet that walked on him. No wonder they are all drinking champaign when the black male is in jail. The black woman is at the beck and call of these white decision makers because of their poverty and their need to survive. They are being controlled in the factory, in the office, in the field and sometimes these women even end up in the bed of these men in some cheap hotel.

Race-betterment in itself is an abstract word. Does this mean that the Pioneer Fund would make over the races and be like a little god? Or does it mean that they would carry out the plan set by the so-called Pilgrims? Documenting and legalizing the inferiority of the Blackman. One day you may access through your computer, and the information on your screen will read: The Blackman has the smallest head, larger genitals and no brains, and every school kid may read that.

25

The black Americans are still talking about unity, while killing each other. Still waiting for role models and political solutions while they are away from their God. When you place the African Americans alongside their white counterpart they are bound to come out inferior, because today they **follow the white man**, instead of leading him as they did before.We confuse ourselves in the search for our own identity, hereby supplying others with the material to label us.

The Blackman of the Americas should have known that he is the true descendants of the children of Israel. Instead he just sees himself as a Blackman and identifies himself with all other black people of the earth, and this is among the first mistakes made. Other Blackmen of the earth were considered always as being different from the children of Israel.

God took Abraham (a Blackman) out of his country Babylon (Chaldea), out of his family (Tribe of Shem), blessed him, and made him great among all fathers of the earth yet made Babylon His enemy. God took Isaac out of his family, all the children of Abraham, including Ishmael and separated him for the covenant. God took Jacob (Israel) out of his family including Esau (Edom) and blessed him with the covenant, made him his first born to inherit a father's inheritance and at the same time hated his brother Esau. God took Moses (adopted Egyptian) out of Egypt to lead the children of Israel out of Egypt, while He hated the Egyptians. God took His people out of the black lands of Ethiopia, Chaldea, Egypt Canaan, cursed the inhabitants of those lands and blessed His people. Yet today the Forgotten Israelites cling to these cursed lands for their identity just because they too are black. Ethiopia was given for ransom to the children of Israel and identified as the enemy. This was also why Miriam was angry at Moses for marrying one, because at that time the Ethiopians were all Ishmeelites and the original Ishmeelites were the Egyptians. That was why the Egyptians and the Ethiopians were always identified together spiritually and physically.

Isaiah 45:14 "Thus saith the Lord, the labour of Egypt, and merchandise of Ethiopia and of the Sabeans, men of stature, shall come over unto thee, and they shall be thine: THEY SHALL COME AFTER THEE, IN CHAINS THEY SHALL COME OVER, AND THEY SHALL FALL DOWN UNTO THEE, THEY SHALL MAKE SUPPLICATION UNTO THEE, saying, Surely God is in thee; and there is none else, there is no God"

You would just have to look at all that is happening today and see with your own eyes and be aware. When you are suppose to be taking up your leadership role and teaching these nations about your God, you end up praising these cursed nations; all in the name of identity. If the Forgotten Israelites need identity, then for God's sake look in your BIBLE not Africa. Zephaniah 2:12-13 "Ye Ethiopians also, ye shall be slain by my sword. And he will stretch out his hand against the north, and destroy Assyria; and will make Nineveh a desolation, and dry like a wilderness."

The Forgotten Israelites should realize that the more they make it an issue of colour the more the enemy rejoices. Look at Africa today, a continent of lost hope, despair, hunger and depression. A people whose spiritual cries have not been heard. Yet among the tears and chaos one leader among these nations took 140 million dollars of his country's money and built a Christian church on the Ivory Coast. This black African placed within the walls of his prized Christian church, a parade of white pictures. A prize for the Pope or other white Christian leaders. Meanwhile his people need bread. What kind of leadership is this for you the Forgotten Israelites to follow? What kind of a nation is this for you to be proud of? A black nation having its own people praising the Gentiles and their gods.

This nation is among those which we were plucked out of, and sold into slavery. Similarly our undying love for the Ishmeelites (Muslims) who sold our Fathers into slavery to the white Christians. Neither of them hold our interest at heart. Yet if we're not a part of one, we are a part of the other.

It is not an issue of colour, the issue is one of power, and it is for this cause that the enemy of the Forgotten Israelites go out of their way to make the African Americans zero. To disqualify them in every aspect of education. To degrade them in every form of intelligence. To deal them unfit as their social equal. To make them the lowest form of human beings. In other words, to make them so inferior, that not even an over-watered dog would see them fit enough to raise his hind legs at.

History taught us that the Israelites had shown the Egyptians the power of their God. Today the new Egyptians are showing the Israelites the power of theirs. The Israelites of old in bondage, never bowed to the Egyptian gods, but longed for the God of their fathers to take them out of bondage.

27

The Israelites today still in bondage, are bowing lower to the gods of the Egyptians and they know not the God of their Fathers. These sons and daughters of slaves have put the spirits of their fathers in a dark place and have forgotten them.

You who call yourself by other names, you who have adopted strange fathers, you who are bastards in the stranger's house, you who dwell in a new household, who have become students instead of teachers, who have chastised my Father. Please DON'T CALL ME BROTHER.

The West Indian Connection

One can understand the Afro American's plight, but what about the Caribbean? In the Caribbean black people are their own bosses, so what is the problem there?

The same excuse. Economic control by the white nations. While this could be part truth, or can be proven through records, it is still not the ultimate reason for this incredible failure. If only politicians and educators could look deeper, black people everywhere in the new world would have a better life. With so many experts in the world today, how come none of them have ever come up with the real solution to the problem? This is because they fail to see that the Blackman's problem happens to be a spiritual one.

Please note that it was the same ship that brought slaves to the U.S. and the Caribbean. These slaves came from the same family. One brother in Barbados, the next in New Orleans. Even George Washington exchanged slaves from Barbados. One cousin in Grenada, the other in Trinidad. Jamaica had split families with Cuba. Guyana with Barbados etc.

All these countries eventually gained independence from the British, but that's all they gained, apart from the knowledge of being ex-slaves. Now they control their own destiny, leading to the path of doom. They all still worship the white gods. These countries are now led by black Christian leaders with the same spiritual philosophy that enslaved their parents before them. Those who control their own land have reduced it to ruin and those that have adopted the white man's land are also in ruin and poverty strickened. Just like the days of old when the Israelites had to go to Egypt for food, black people are now fleeing in large numbers to the United States, Britain and Canada in search of a better life. So the black family that was once separated is slowly getting together again, waiting for Moses; but the Moses of today is the spirit of truth.

Here is a breakdown of the richness of some the nations in the Caribbean amid the ruins of a dream, where strong men are now made weak, where proud men are now made to be humble, where the milk is now sour and the honey is no more.

Trinidad and Tobago

Trinidad is about 1,864 square miles. Tobago is about 116 square miles. This country produces petroleum, which started with the British and the Dutch in the early 1900s. After the Second World War the United States helped to develop this industry which is found in the southern part of the island and off shore in the Gulf of Paria. This industry has by-products such as natural gas, cement, natural asphalt of world class quality, and even fertilizer.

In agriculture this country produces sugar cane, cocoa, citrus fruits, coffee, coconut etc. Yet in the 1990s Trinidad and Tobago is among the poorest in the Caribbean.

Guyana

This country is 83,000 square miles in size. It produces bauxite (among the best in the world), has the potential to produce manganese and uranium, vast amounts of diamonds and gold were discovered in this country which also produces rice, citrus fruits, ground provisions, sugar cane. Guyana means land of many waters. A land with three main rivers, plus other smaller ones, creeks and lakes. Yet Guyana still has a lot of trouble in the 90s supplying drinking water to its citizens. This country also has a vast forest of fine woods including the hard wood Greenheart. A once rich country populated with proud people, is now in extreme poverty.

Jamaica

This land is the third largest island of the Caribbean, after Cuba and Hispaniola (Haiti and The Dominican Republic); which together with Puerto Rico is known as the Greater Antilles. This island is situated five hundred miles southeast of the United States and ninety miles south of Cuba. It also has fertile soil which grows cacao, spices, citrus, bananas etc. Also produces world class bauxite. At the end of Jamaica's four hundred years it's citizens are still struggling to survive.

Barbados

This island is known, as far back as I can remember, as little England. Again this island can produce all the tropical fruits and vegetables mentioned in other countries of the region, plus it has beautiful sandy beaches.

These are the frontline of the Caribbean states, all of which, with all their great potential FAILED. Are these countries really independent without the money from the former slave owners? Without the money from tourism, grants and loans, or the IMF they could not have survived. Why did this group of nations fail to come together for a common cause as a family? It was no coincident that the one member state that refused to be joined was Jamaica. Please note the end of Jamaica's 400 years was early 1900s (See The Truth The Lie and The Bible). The spiritual bond was not there, so it could never happen.

Everything that happens to Israelites today has a spiritual meaning. The most outstanding evidence is the poverty that they live and dwell in, even though they are surrounded by so much wealth. Because they have turned away from the God of their fathers. Now they are all Christians serving a white and false god and proud of it.

Here are some Forgotten Israelites in the new Egypt; past and present. Malcolm X (parent-Grenada). Louis Farrakhan (parent-St. Kitts). Colin Powell (parents-Jamaica).

We need not go further down in history. These three men are all outstanding Americans. So when we are talking about Blackmen (Israelites) we are talking about the children of slaves in the Americas, from the time the history of the Forgotten Israelites began to unfold in Portugal in the 15th century right down to the last slave today (for mental slavery is far worse than physical bondage).

In some cultures in Latin America the people drink blood, the blood of goats and other animals. They worship in all the pagan ways and practice voodoo and obeah under the shades of Christianity. This is part of dressing up the devilish lie with skimpy garments of truth. Some outrightly reject the truth. Some cover their ears.

There is a reason why one with the knowledge of truth, would get extremely emotional by just looking at the ignorance being

31

displayed by some Forgotten Israelites in the region of the Americas, like the Israelites of old as is written in I Kings 22:17 "And he said, I saw all Israel scattered upon the hills, as sheep that have not a shepherd: and the Lord said. These have no master; Let them return every man to his house in peace".

This scripture pleas with the children of Israel to return to their house, meaning old ways of acknowledging the God of their fathers again. If we continue to read further, we might be able to understand why the lies are more appealing to God's people today than the truth. You will find the answer in the same chapter, the 21st - 23rd verse. "And there came forth a spirit, and stood before the Lord, and said, I will persuade him.

And the Lord said unto him, Wherewith? And he said, I will go forth, and I will be A LYING SPIRIT IN THE MOUTH OF HIS PROPHETS. And he said, Thou shalt persuade him, and prevail also; go forth and do so.

Now therefore, behold, THE LORD HATH PUT A LYING SPIRIT IN THE MOUTH OF ALL THESE THY PROPHETS, and the Lord hath spoken evil concerning thee."

They are all like sheep gone astray and it is such a shame that a people so rich in the spirit would turn all of it over to darkness, destruction and despair.

WHO IS AN ISRAELITE?

An Israelite is not a follower - He is a leader
An Israelite is not a student - He is a teacher
An Israelite does the will of God.
An Israelite could not be wrong
An Israelite doesn't kiss a boot - He is of the truth
An Israelite is not black - An Israelite is not white
He's not a Muslim nor Christian He's right
He keeps the laws, the statutes and commandments
He's strong in God, spirit and self
No Israelite should bend his knee
No Israelite in poverty

No Israelite should walk in vain
No Israelite should be ashamed
Love God Love self Your brethren too
Love all Not world Just close to you
Reach out to help the one that's near
Look up for help and He'll be there
Brethren means brother and sister too
Israelite means God's chosen me and you
No other path to follow in this world
No other God that man should call
There's no god from the east No god out west
Like the God of Israel cause He's the best
The God of our Fathers looks down on us
The God of Abraham, Isaac and Jacob
Don't listen what the world's saying
Don't listen Don't listen to lies
They're strong in numbers but that's all they've got
We got knowledge and power on our side
And when the curtain is drawn and night is come
When all is over and you lie down
It would be to sleep and not to die
Cause you are of the truth, not of the lie
And when your name is called in the Book of Life
You'll say Thank God Almighty I'm an Israelite

The lost tribes of the children of Israel travelled through the
Mediterranean, the Middle East and Africa and co-habited with
these nations just as the bible had predicted. Hereby making some
of these white skinned people direct descendants. You should not
hate the white man, but teach him. Do not worship his god,
because he has no god of power, comparing to your God. Why
do you not understand what your fathers went through? Why is it
when you get the knowledge of truth you turn it to the knowledge
of hatred? You turn it around to hate the white man, who is a

confused man without a culture that is uniquely his. What about the white man who died so that you could live? What about the abolitionists? Do you think the answer lies in your hatred for the white man? No!

You are teaching him even now and not knowing it. So why not let him know. Remember when your fathers were playing jazz? The white man knew nothing of it. He tried as hard as he could, but he still couldn't play it. Then you taught him, and went on to sing and play blues and gospel. Again he tried hard to be like you and ended up singing country. Then you moved to soul. He followed you there too. In the 1990s he is telling himself that he is the number one soul singer in the persons of Michael McDonald, George Michael, Michael Bolton and a host of others, along with the New Kids on the Block. But he knows deep down inside that he can never, not in a million years be like you, so he created a system whereby you can automatically be disqualified according to his rules. You have now moved. You are now rapping, and if you look over your shoulder you'll find him. You taught him to slap the palm, now he's doing it better than you. You taught him slang like "right on" etc. These are just a few of today's situations. Think about what you taught him in the past, things that you have forgotten.

He has been a very good student, but you, a reluctant teacher. It's time you teach him about your God, for the time is right. He was too scared of your spiritual strength in the old years, but now that you are weaker, he is not afraid. Take hold of your spirituality again while you still have some left.

It is true that evil comes in the shape and appearance of the white man, as written in the scriptures, but please do not forget that other Blackmen were once your enemies too (the Egyptians and the Canaanites). Your true enemy are not Christians but CHRISTIANITY, which is a philosophy of the white man. You should now take over the role of the father figure and teacher.

Even though Islam is not your enemy you must realize that it was the Muslims who sold your fathers to Christians. Joseph learned to forgive his brothers, but our situation is by far different. Joseph and his brothers were Israelites of the same family. Our fathers, who were made slaves and the Muslims were just related and not the whole family, like Joseph and his brothers.

The story of Joseph is written in Genesis 37:23-28 "And it came to pass, when Joseph was come unto his brethren, that they

34

stript Joseph out of his coat, his coat of many colours that was on him.

And they took him and cast him in to a pit: and the pit was empty, there was no water in it.

And they sat down to eat bread: and they lifted up their eyes and looked: and behold, a company of ISHMEELITES came from Gilead with their camels bearing spicery and balm and myrrh, going to carry it down to Egypt.

And Judah said unto his brethren, What profit is it if we slay our brother, and conceal his blood?

Come, and let us sell him to the ISHMEELITES, and let not our hand be upon him: for he is our brother and our flesh. And His brethren were content.

Then there passed by Midianites, merchantmen: and they drew and lifted up Joseph out of the pit, and sold Joseph to the ISHMEELITES for twenty pieces of silver: and they brought Joseph into Egypt."

Let's read now to see who Joseph still showed his love for. Genesis 45:1-5 "Then Joseph could not refrain himself before all them that stood by him: and he cried, Cause every man to go out from me. And there stood no man with him, while Joseph made himself known unto his BRETHREN.

And he wept aloud: and the Egyptians and the house of Pharaoh heard.

And Joseph said unto his brethren, I am Joseph: doth my father yet live? And his brethren could not answer him: for they were troubled at his presence.

And Joseph said unto his brethren, come near to me, I pray you. And they came near. And he said, I am Joseph your brother, whom ye SOLD INTO EGYPT.

Now therefore be not grieved, nor angry with yourselves, that ye sold me hither: for God did sent me before you to preserve life."

In today's situation, Islam is a descendant from Ishmael, a half brother, whose mother was Hagar, an Egyptian, whose people became the enemy of our fathers (The Israelites). It was the Egyptians who enslaved the Israelites, just like the Muslims who sold them to Christians as slaves. God had given us a personal covenant to keep, which is far more important than a mere blessing that he gave to Ishmael.

35

God has chosen us, the Israelites, for His own people. Doesn't that mean something? Why still hold on to a dream, when reality could be like milk and honey. Remember Joseph had the same rights as the rest of his brothers. Ishmael was an outcast and did not share in the covenant as is proven in the scriptures.

Let's now turn to the scriptures for it is with the scriptures that the truth would be known to God's people. To prove that black people in the Americas are the true Israelites we must first prove that the old Israelites were black, then trace their journey from Israel to North Africa, to the Iberian Peninsula and to Western Africa, where they were sold into slavery, then to the Americas as slaves again. According to the scriptures the Israelites would see the land of Israel no more, but Edom (the children of Esau - Edomites) would return and build.

To prove that God's people were black, let's first look at their characteristics, attitude, culture, then their colour and hair texture. Any farmer knows that black soil is the best soil, and the Garden of Eden was the best of the rest. Genesis 2:7 "And the Lord God formed man of the dust of the ground and breathed into his nostrils the breath of life and man became a living soul."

Now if this soil was the best then it had to be black. Therefore the first man was black. The next stage is very clear. God said that the man whom he had made was like unto Him, because He made Him in His own IMAGE (like a human being) and LIKENESS (resemblance in every way). Genesis 1:27 "So God created man in His own image, in the image of God created he him, male and female created He them."

If we turn back to verse 26 we would find that the first man was not only in the image of God, but also His likeness. "And God said, Let us make man in our image, after our likeness and let them have dominion of the fish of the sea, and over the fowl of the air, and over the cattle and over all the earth, and over every creeping thing that creepeth upon the earth."

I have proven through the scriptures that the first man was black, made in the image and likeness of God, of whom I will continue to prove at the time of creation was black. (See The Truth The Lie and The Bible - In Search of the Other Family).

Let's now look at the characteristics of our God, the God of our Fathers. In the eyes of men, when you have red eyes or brown, big noses, thick lips, woolly hair etc. you are classified as an African or a black person.

36

In Revelations 1:14 it describes the coming of Jesus the Christ. Here is the description: "His head and His hairs were white like wool as white as snow and his eyes are as a flame of fire." You can see an old man with grey hair (white - woolly) with red eyes. When you read what it said in Genesis 2:7 He (God) must have had a big nose.

Genesis 7:22 "All in whose NOSTRILS was the breath of life of all that was in the dry land died." Exodus 15:8 "And with the blast of thy NOSTRILS the waters were gathered together, the floods stood upright as an heap, and the depths were congealed in the heart of the sea." II Samuel 22:9 "There went up a smoke out of his NOSTRILS and fire out of his mouth devoured coals were kindled by it." Psalm 18:8 &15

Let's us now satisfy ourselves and confirm the fact of this main characteristic. Job 4:9 By the blast of God, they perish and by the breath of his NOSTRILS are they consumed." We know through the past scriptures that He is black with red eyes, thick lips, a big nose and woolly hair.

Daniel 7:9 "I beheld till the thrones were cast down and the Ancient of Days did sit whose garment was white as snow and the hair of his head like the pure WOOL, his throne was like the fiery flame and his wheels as burning fire."

All the characteristics of our God were inherited by His people in Job 30:30, Jeremiah 8:21, Lamentation 4:8. Paul was called a nigger in Acts 13:1. He was also called an Egyptian in Acts 21:38. It was the woolly hair that the Ethiopians, Egyptians and Israelites plaited (weaved) with gold or as a simple way of holding it in one piece. Straight hair cannot hold together in a plait for long. This was a fashion that the Greeks stole from the Egyptians who were masters at fashion. Note even lipstick and cheek colours were invented in Egypt.

To prove this point of the plaiting of the hair. Read I Peter 3:3 "Whose adorning let it not be that outward adorning of plaiting of hair and of wearing of gold or of putting on of apparel." Peter is referring to the custom of the people while explaining that none of these things will help, only the hidden purity of the heart. Read it in verse 4.

We have dealt with the appearance and looks of God and His people. Let's confirm it in Genesis 35:10 "And God said unto Him thy name is Jacob. Thy name shall not be called anymore

Jacob but ISRAEL shall be thy name and he called his name Israel." For the complete story read (The Story of Israel in The Truth The Lie and The Bible) or Genesis 25 & 49. Let's find out now about Ishmael and his relationship with the Israelites of old, or Islam and the Israelites of today, but first let us examine in a logical way the word HATE as being used today by BLACK PEOPLE.

How can you truly hate the whiteman and report for work in his office, or factory? How can you say you hate the whiteman and still use his money? How can you say you hate the whiteman and be so dependent on his services?

Please let us not kid ourselves. Margus Garvey, Frederick Douglas, and others had this message long before we were born. They all wanted to go back to Africa, which was the best thing to do at that time, to be totally free from the whiteman's domination, but it failed. The ones that went to LIBERIA were not really free either, when you consider the facts. LIBERIA was even importing bread from the United States. Now take a good look at Liberia today.

PHYSICALLY the wealthy Blackman should spend his money to create jobs for his people. He does not. He buys fancy cars, lives in fancy houses, wears expensive jewelry, and makes donations to justify his tax returns. How many factories, manufacturing plants, corporations, and industries does he own and how many of his people has he employed?

When the Blackman with all his wealth and power, begins to do these things, it would be a step in the right direction. Right now he is a master at excuses, and he is even believing them. Our leaders sit in their fancy communities telling you about black history, while silently engaging in all the ways of making money for themselves. When there is no food to eat, history or the knowledge of it cannot satisfy you, and this is where your SPIRITUALITY comes in.

FIGHT IN THIS WORLD FOR YOUR ECONOMIC POWER THEN TURN TO YOUR GOD FOR SPIRITUAL STRENGHT.

KEEP THE LAWS OF THE GOD OF ISRAEL AND NOTHING WILL STOP YOU. DO NOT RELY ON HATE. IT FAILED BEFORE, IT IS FAILING NOW, AND IT WILL CONTINUE TO FAIL.

EDOM AND ISRAEL
ISLAM AND CHRISTIANITY

It is said that Islam, or the generation of Ishmael, is the obedient one! TRUE. Genesis tells you of the birth of today's generations, descendants from SHEM, HAM and JAPHETH. There are only three races divided up into tribes and nations, but all are from these Blackmen.

Let's now look at the relationship of these three men and these FOUR CULTURES - Ishmael, Israel, Edom and Christianity-the-impostor. You would find that Edom (Esau) is related to Israel (Jacob) and Islam (Ishmael) is related to Israel also. That leaves Christianity without a base, without a foundation, without a root and without substance. Christianity can officially be called a thief, a liar and a crook. Nowhere in the foundation of biblical history is Christianity mentioned as an original religion. As a matter of fact it is not mentioned as a statue, law or a commandment, or in any way connected: yet suddenly out of the blue comes a white god, with no background, no history and no substance, yet he is the most powerful god of the world, like Santa Claus and Christmas, where everyone adores this false god, even Israelites.

Here is some brief historical facts about Christianity. Christianity, or the teachers of this pagan religion claim that it originated from the Holy Bible, yet if you looked closely at the customs of this Roman institutionalized organization, you will find the use of biblical names, but pagan ways and practices.

Let's take a look at this most influential religious weapon. The laws and customs of the people in Israel were very secured after they returned from Babylon 50 years after their captivity. They remained in peace as they rebuilt Jerusalem, until 333 B.C. This was when the Greeks ruled over Israel, then the Egyptians for a short while until 167 B.C., then Judah Macabee started a rebellion and regained control of the Jewish temples in Jerusalem: and Macabee was as dark as his fathers before him, and with woolly hair. This independence was kept until 37 B.C. when the Romans came. The destruction of the dark race was at its highest peak. Battle after battle was fought and eventually in 70 A.D. the destruction of the temples of Jerusalem by the Romans. By this time they had already killed prominent Israelites that they claim now to be serving today. Among them was Jesus, who was nailed to the cross by Roman soldiers, not Jews. They had already taken off the head of John the Baptist, and in 67 A.D. the head of Paul. They jailed Peter, and thereby started the destruction of the Israelites, while implementing their own custom on the people, calling them Christians.

From this time until the sixteenth century, Rome, along with the help of Greece, Germany, Britain and Spain managed to keep God's people under control, both body and mind. They then began the enslavement of God's people again, and the prophecy of the 400 years began its unfolding.

They have managed successfully to clothe the lie with some truth. They would praise Paul even though they killed him, but they would say that he was a Christian, when he was an Israelite. The first Pope of Rome was called Peter, so that you would believe that he was the man of God, when he was not. Most of them were called saints, when they were not even qualified for the job. None of them were spiritually equipped according to the scriptures, to be called saints.

The confusion continued down through the ages. At the end of the 4th century rich Christians of Rome took up permanent residence in Palestine. Meanwhile the Christian church developed a new word called THEOLOGY, and the men who wrote this theology of the church were called fathers. All the Christian laws of the day were written in Greek and Latin. The word saint was used to separate these men from others. It had absolutely nothing to do with the saints written about in the bible.

In the fifteenth century opposition was on the rise. Leonardo da Vinci (1452-1519) and Desiderius Erasmus (1466-1536) were among the first to rebel openly. In those days there was much talk, about money, and the big business of the church. The God of Israel was never mentioned. The theologians had created laws that said when you commit a sin under their law, you must pay money to the church, and your sins would be forgiven. More rebellion came as church leaders began to make new laws to suit themselves.

On October 31st, 1517 a Catholic priest Martin Luther said that he disagreed with most of what the Christians were doing, and said it was not according to the doctrine of saint Paul. Please note, not God, but Paul. In France was yet another, his name was John Calvin. He was born in the north of France, a writer and

40

Christian organizer. In 1536 he wrote a book called "The Institutes". This short history of the Christian church should open your minds to a fuller understanding of this pagan religion, and the confusion of it all. You would discover how the real God was hijacked and replaced by these men, who in turn played God.

There is no substance in the Christian church, only the practising of sophisticated WITCHCRAFT. All Christian churches worship the dead, and all Christian churches are children of the Catholic Church. The Christian church is the enemy of God. The chosen of God will never find salvation in these institutions.

This prediction is very obvious in the scriptures. It tells of how great Christianity would become that the entire world would admire her. The Great Whore! Revelation 17:6 "And I saw the woman drunken with the blood of the saints, and with the blood of the martyrs of Jesus: and when I saw her, I wondered with **GREAT ADMIRATION."**

Here is how God had chosen His people through the scriptures. Genesis 12:1-3 "Now the Lord had said unto ABRAM, Get thee out of thy country, and from thy kindred, and from thy father's house, unto a land that I will shew thee: And I will make of thee a great nation, and I will bless thee, and make thy name great: and thou shalt be a blessing: And I will bless them that bless thee, and curse him that curseth thee: and in thee shall all families of the earth be blessed." This scripture proves that God took Abram away from a world that was already in existence, for there were others outside the family of Abram and out of Abram's family itself Abram was chosen. These facts would put to shame the notion that Abraham was the father of all people.

Let's find the scriptures to Abram's identity. First his father. Genesis 11:26-28 "And Terah lived seventy years, and begat Abram, Nahor, and Haran. Now these are the generations of Terah: Terah begat Abram, Nahor, and Haran; and Haran begat Lot. And Haran died before his father Terah, in the land of his nativity, in Ur of the Chaldees." It was Abram and his family who travelled the region. In Chapter 12 the Lord spoke to him, giving him instructions to get out of his father's house because of the plan that the Almighty God had for him. Genesis 15:7 "And he said unto him, I am the Lord that brought thee out of Ur of the Chaldees, to give thee this land to inherit it." Nehemiah 9:7 "Thou art the Lord thy God, who didst choose Abram, and broughest him forth out of Ur of the Chaldees, and gavest him the name of

Abraham;"

Abram was plucked out of the tribe of Shem, so he had to be like his fathers before him, black! While the others of the tribe of Shem formed the EAST INDIAN type race that travelled and lived all over India, Persia and Arabia. They might not be known as East Indians outside of India, because of tribal differences and other nationalities which started way back from the Tower of Babel.

Let's now get the whole story of Islam (Ishmael). Genesis 16:1-16 "Now Sarai, Abram's wife bare him no children: and she had an handmaid, an EGYPTIAN, whose name was Hagar.
And Sarai said unto Abram, Behold now, the Lord hath restrained me from bearing: I pray thee, go in unto my maid; it may be that I may obtain children by her. And Abram hearkened to the voice of Sarai.
And Sarai, Abram's wife took Hagar her maid the Egyptian, after Abram had dwelt ten years in the land of Canaan, and gave her to her husband Abram to be his WIFE.
And He went in unto Hagar, and she conceived: and when she saw that she had conceived, her mistress was despised in her eyes.
And Sarai said unto Abram, My wrong be upon thee: I have given my maid into thy bosom; and when she saw that she had conceived, I was despised in her eyes: The Lord judge between me and thee.
But Abram said unto Sarai, Behold, thy maid is in thy hand; do to her as it pleaseth thee. And when Sarai dealt hardly with her, she fled from her face. And the angel of the Lord found her by a fountain of water in the wilderness, by the fountain in the way to Shur.
And he said, Hagar, Sarai's maid, whence camest thou? and whither wilt thou go? And she said, I flee from the face of my mistress Sarai.
And the angel of the Lord said unto her. Return to thy mistress, and submit thyself under her hands.
And the angel of the Lord said unto her, I will multiply thy seed exceedingly, that it shall not be numbered for multitude.
And the angel of the Lord said unto her, Behold, thou art with child, and shalt bear a son, and shalt call his name ISHMAEL; because the Lord hath heard thy affliction.
And he will be a wild man; his hand will be against every man,

42

and every man's hand against him; and he shall dwell in the presence of all his brethren.

And she called the name of the Lord that spake unto her, Thou God seeth me for she said, Have I also here looked after him that seeth me?

Wherefore the well was called Beerlahairoi; behold, it is between Kadesh and Bered.

And Hagar bare Abram a son: and Abram called his son's name, which Hagar bare, ISHMAEL.

And Abram was fourscore and six years old, when Hagar bare ISHMAEL to Abram." This is the story of Ishmael of whom the very foundation of Islam was built.

THE TRANSFORMATION OF ABRAM

Genesis 17:1-10 "And when Abram was ninety years old and nine, the Lord appeared to Abram, and said unto him, I am the Almighty God; walk before me, and be thou perfect.

And I will make my covenant between me and thee, and will multiply thee exceedingly.

And Abram fell on his face: and God talked with him, saying.

As for me, behold my covenant is with thee, and thou shalt be a father of many nations.

Neither shall thy name anymore be called Abram, but thy name shall be ABRAHAM; for a father of many nations have I made thee.

And I will make thee exceeding fruitful, and I will make nations of thee, and kings shall come out of thee.

And I will establish my covenant between me and thee and thy seed after thee in their generations for an everlasting covenant, to be a God unto thee, and to thy seed after thee.

And I will give unto thee, and to thy seed after thee, the land wherein thou art a stranger, all the land of Canaan, for an everlasting possession; and I will be their God.

And God said unto Abraham, Thou shalt keep my covenant therefore, thou and thy seed after thee in their generations.

This is my covenant, which ye shall keep, between me and you

43

and thy seed after thee; EVERY MAN CHILD AMONG YOU SHALL BE CIRCUMCISED."

Verse 15-24 "And God said unto Abraham, As for Sarai thy wife, thou shalt not call her name Sarai, but Sarah shall her name be.

And I will bless her, and give thee a son also of her: yea, I will bless her, and she shall be a mother of nations; kings of people shall be of her.

Then Abraham fell upon his face, and laughed, and said in his heart, Shall a child be born unto him that is an hundred years old? and shall Sarah, that is ninety years old, bear?

And Abraham said unto God, O that ISHMAEL might live before thee!

And God said, Sarah thy wife shall bear thee a son indeed; and thou shalt call his name ISAAC: and I will establish my covenant with him for an everlasting covenant, and with his seed after him.

And as for ISHMAEL, I have heard thee: behold I have blessed him and will make him fruitful, and will multiply him exceedingly; twelve princes shall he beget, and I will make him a great nation.

But my covenant will I establish with Isaac, which Sarah shall bear unto thee at this set time in the next year.

And he left off talking with him, and God went up from Abraham. And Abraham took Ishmael his son, and all that were born in his house, and all that were bought with his money, every male among the men of Abraham's house; and circumcised the flesh of their foreskin in the self same day, as God had said unto him.

And Abraham was ninety years old and nine, when he was circumcised in the flesh of his foreskin."

Now let's try to analyse what had happened so far. First, Abram planted his seed in an Egyptian woman Hagar. She gave birth to a son ISHMAEL. God had blessed this son and gave him princes and wealth in his nations, but then God performed a miracle by allowing Sarah to be pregnant and said that it will be with this child that He would establish His covenant: NOT ISHMAEL. The first son of Abram was Ishmael, but the first son of Abraham was ISAAC. Note that God had spiritually transformed ABRAM to ABRAHAM. This was a sign of a relationship that was meant to change the course of life itself. The changing of his name had given Abram a spiritual birth. After he had spiritually changed him, a bond was created between Abraham and God through circumcision. Then with this spiritual purity Isaac was born and this is the difference between the two sons.

44

Now let's get back to the scriptures and clarify this misconception often used by the children of slavery, that all black people are Muslims. Not so at all, all the children of slavery are ISRAELITES.

THE BIRTH OF ISAAC

Genesis 21:1-4 "And the Lord visited Sarah as he had said, and the Lord did unto Sarah as he had spoken.

For Sarah conceived, and bare Abraham a son in his old age, at the set time of which God had spoken to him.

And Abraham called the name of his son that was born unto him, whom Sarah bare to him, Isaac.

And Abraham circumcised his son Isaac being eight days old, as God had commanded him.

Verses 9-13 "And Sarah saw the son of Hagar the Egyptian, which she had born unto Abraham, mocking.

Wherefore she said unto Abraham, Cast out this bondwoman and her son: for the son of this bondwoman shall not be heir with my son, even with Isaac.

And the thing was very grievous in Abraham's sight because of his son.

And God said unto Abraham, Let it not be grievous in thy sight because of the lad, and because of thy bondwoman; in all that Sarah hath said unto thee, hearken unto her voice; FOR IN ISAAC SHALL THY SEED BE CALLED. And also of the son of the bondwoman will I make a nation, because he is thy seed."

Here is where the scriptures are very clear. The covenant will be with Isaac and not ISHMAEL, for Ishmael's blessing has come true. Egypt was the greatest of all nations upon this earth. From Ishmael's seed came great men. The religion of Islam practised by all the nations surrounding Egypt today is indeed powerful. He (Ishmael) is rich, for all of the world accepts Islam as fruit out of the root of ISHMAEL.

Mohamed was a Blackman, who claimed that he was the descendant of ISHMAEL, the EGYPTIAN. The proof is clear only for people with eyes to see and ears to hear. Mohamed transferred most of what was already written in the bible by our fathers. His wife being an Israelite also helped him to write the Koran. From Ishmael to Mohamed none of whom could have made it without the help of our Fathers, THE ISRAELITES.

45

THE BIRTH OF EDOM AND ISRAEL

Genesis 25:20-26 "And Isaac was forty years old when he took Rebekah to wife, the daughter of Bethuel the Syrian of Padanaram, the sister of Laban the Syrian. And Isaac intreated the Lord for his wife, because she was barren: and the Lord was intreated of him, and Rebekah his wife conceived.

And the children struggled together within her, and she said, If it be so, why am I thus? And she went to inquire of the Lord.

And the Lord said unto her, Two nations are in thy womb, and two manner of people shall be separated from thy bowels; and the one people shall be stronger than the other people; and the elder shall serve the younger.

And when her days to be delivered were fulfilled, behold, there were twins in her womb.

And the first came out RED, all over like an hairy garment; and they called his name Esau.

And after that came his brother out, and his hand took hold on Esau's heel; and his name was called Jacob: And Isaac was threescore years old when she bare them."

Let's now find out who was called EDOM. Genesis 36:1 "Now these are the generations of ESAU, WHO IS EDOM." Let's find out further who is Israel. Genesis 35:10 "And God said unto him, Thy name is Jacob: thy name shall not be called any more Jacob, but ISRAEL shall be thy name: and he called his name ISRAEL." According to scriptures we have identified men who are the background or backbone of today's religions. Yet we have not seen Christianity.

Out of EDOM comes the religion that today call themselves Jews, who are white people, and nowhere is it written that the colour of the Jews changed from black to white.

In the 15th century Pope Julius II ordered Michelangelo to paint all biblical heroes WHITE. The scriptures are very clear in its description of EDOM. If we read what has been said in the Holy Bible we would discover that the baby Esau came out red, and the white man is not as white as this paper you're reading from, but closer to red. I rest my case. Nevertheless, there is that relationship of brother, not so much brotherhood. Because of the similarity of our back ground and history it is almost impossible not to notice that the Arians, Ku Klux Klan and other Christians never can hate one and love the other. It is as though we both

46

came out of the same mould. Everyone that hates the Blackman hates the Jews (Edomites). The Christian teachers preach from their pulpits every Sunday about love, and how God loves everybody, yet we find the ones who teach this, do not practice it. The Israelite teaching is that God does not love everybody. God loves those who follow His laws, statues, and commandments. God loves those who love the children of Israel, so the doctrine of God loving everyone is wrong.

The scripture tells of God's hatred for Edom, but nevertheless He blessed him with riches because of his father, Isaac. Have you ever noticed that no one in today's society call themselves EDOMITES? Here's why.

First, Edom tried to darken the skin of his generations by intermingling with Ishmael. Genesis 28:9 "Then went Esau unto ISHMAEL, and took unto the wives which he had Mahalath the daughter of Ishmael Abraham's son, the sister of Nebajoth, to be his wife".

Even with all of this they still seem to be out of place in the region today for everyone else is a shade darker. God even told Jacob to flee from his face. Genesis 35:1 "And God said unto Jacob, Arise, go up to Bethel, and dwell there: and make there an altar unto God, that appeared unto thee when thou fleddest from the face of Esau thy brother." Though they were brothers in the flesh, one was spiritually rich, while the other became materially rich. Deut. 2:5 "Meddle not with them; for I will not give you of their land, no, not so much as a foot breadth; because I have given mount Seir unto Esau for a possession."

Here again is the separation because of spiritual differences; one with and the other without. Malachi 1:2-5 "I have loved you saith the Lord, Yet ye say, wherein hast thou loved us? Was not Esau Jacob's brother? saith the Lord: yet I loved Jacob.
And I hated ESAU, and laid his mountains and his heritage waste for the dragons of the wilderness.
Whereas Edom saith, We are impoverished, but we will return and build the desolate places; thus saith the Lord of hosts, They shall build, but I will throw down; and they shall call them, The border of wickedness, and, The people against whom the Lord hath indignation for ever.
And your eyes shall see, and ye shall say, The Lord will be magnified from the border of Israel."

Today the world believes, especially Christians who

desperately need a god, that the present day Israel is the holy land, how holy can this land be? This land was cursed, and left desolate by God's people until Edom came in 1948, just as the bible predicted in Malachi. God said that they would build but He would throw it down. The world can see this happening, yet cannot understand.

The scriptures say that God will be magnified from the borders of Israel, not inside Israel but outside. The first land of Israel was named after Jacob, the first son of God.

Exodus 4:22 "And thou shalt say unto Pharaoh, Thus saith the Lord, Israel is my son, even my first born:"

This Israel is named by man. The first land of Israel had the twelve sons of Jacob's offspring. Today the land of Israel is confused about this understanding. The first people of Israel were educated in Egypt, and came out of EGYPT.

Hosea 11:1 "When Israel was a child, then I loved him, and called my son out of Egypt."

The people of today's Israel came from Europe. Then what is so difficult for people to understand?

THE MISUNDERSTANDING

The Edomites of Israel are saying that the Falashas are Jews from the Lost Tribe of Dan. Now how can one be a Jew and at the same time be a Danite? This means that someone is ignorant, or is deliberately lying to fool the world again. Jews are from the tribe of Judah, the fourth son of Israel. Genesis 29:35.

The Danites are from the tribe of Dan, the fifth son of Israel. Genesis 30:1-6 That makes it highly impossible to be a Jew from another tribe. If the Falashas are of Dan then they are lying again because so is Samson, yet they want you to believe that God's people are white as portrayed in all of Hollywood's movies. Judges 13:24-25 "And the woman bare a son, and called his name Samson: and the child grew, and the Lord blessed him.

And the Spirit of the Lord began to move him at times in the camp of DAN between Zorah and Eshtaol". See verse 2 for the tribe of SAMSON'S FATHER.

Let's take a close look at the Falashas themselves, or Beta Israel as they are called. Beta Israel means House of Israel and the House of Israel has twelve tribes from Rueben to Benjamin. Some historians say that when the kingdom of Dan was destroyed in and

48

around 722 B.C. the children of Dan trickled to this part of Ethiopia and came with their culture and customs. If this is so, it would explain the reason why the original Jews are like the Ethiopians, BLACK. The one story that is most acceptable is the one that has another place in history, which states that the Falashas are the descendants from the generation of Menelek, who was the son of MAKEDA, the Queen of Sheba and the Jewish King Solomon. This line also went to Queen Judith who was called the Falasha Queen. She ruled over Abyssinia, the other name for Ethiopia, for 40 years. If this story is accurate then they are not of Dan, but rather Jews from the tribe of Judah. If you call them Jews the descendants of Solomon, then who or what will you call the people living in Israel today?

When you study the customs and culture of the Falashas there is more proof that they are the descendants of Israel. These are a people that were taught the old ways through the generations, not in a university. Their customs coincide with those of the old Israel of biblical times.This is really something for you to think about . If history has proven that all the children of Israel were black, then who are these white ones? Revelations 2:9 and Revelations 3:9. Read it for yourselves in your own bible. Remember Jews are not of a religion, but a nation of people, unlike what others would want you to believe. The Israelites are special people called by God Himself.

This chapter can never be closed without the destiny revealed by God to His people, the Israelites. Genesis 15:13 "And he said unto Abram, Know of a surety that thy seed shall be a stranger in a land that is not theirs, and shall serve them; and they shall afflict them four hundred years;"

Please note every 400 years black people have been enslaved from the time of EGYPT. Why? Because we never turned to our God. Deut. 28:43-44 "The stranger that is within thee shall get up above thee very high; and thou shalt come down very low.
He shall lend to thee, and thou shalt not lend to him: He shall be the head, and thou shalt be the tail."

All that the children of slavery need to do, is to take a good look at themselves and the philosophy of their white Christian god. The more Christianized are black people, the greater their burden. They look at other Christians that don't look like them, who are making it, and compare themselves. They don't seem to understand that the philosophy of the Christian church is so high

49

that their capacity to think for themselves is at its minimum. While others are rich, they are poor. Yet they would not leave this strange god alone.

Verse 64 "And the Lord shall scatter thee among all people, from the one end of the earth even unto the other; and there thou shalt serve other gods, which neither thou nor thy fathers have known, even wood and stone."

Black people have been brought to this strange land and they have been worshipping gods their fathers had not known. They have been serving wood (the cross, the symbol of death).

Verse 68 "And the Lord shall bring thee into Egypt again with ships, by the way whereof I spake unto thee, THOU SHALT SEE IT NO MORE AGAIN: and there ye shall be sold unto your enemies for bondmen and bondwomen, and no man shall buy you."

One does not need ships to travel from Israel to Egypt. The scriptures are talking about the slavery to the new world. It also states that you shall see ISRAEL no more. So tell me who lives there when the Israelites would not see it any more? The scriptures are very clear when it says that the Israelites would be taken into slavery AGAIN. Let us now use our common sense. Who was taken into slavery AGAIN and AGAIN after their disobedience to the God of Abraham, the God of Isaac and the God of Jacob? Let me answer this for you. The children of slavery! The black people of the Americans! The Forgotten Israelites!

You might still ask, how come the Egyptians of today are not as black as they used to be, but rather seem to be a mixture of peoples? Here is a bit of history on Egypt, bearing in mind that the Egyptians and the Ethiopians for most part of history shared almost the same cultures. There were at least eighteen to twenty Ethiopian kings that ruled Egypt. They both had believed in the same gods throughout history. They both had also practiced the customs of their father Ishmael. It was in Egypt that the calendar or almanac was invented hereby allowing us to be aware of the moon, the sun and astrology. Here is how EGYPT changed her FACE and culture from the first Egypt.

In 1675 B.C. the Hyksos invaded the country and introduced horses and chariots. The Egyptians fought back and in 1500 B.C. drove the Hyksos out. Between 1000 B.C. and 332 B.C. Egypt was over run by Libya, Ethiopia, Assyria and Persia. In 332 B.C. the Greeks, under Alexander the Great, controlled Egypt through

50

the likeness of General Ptolemy.

The first dynasty ended in 30 B.C. when Cleopatra (69-30 B.C.) took her own life. She was the last of that line. Egypt then went under the control of Rome. About 670 years Egypt was under Roman and Byzantine emperors. It was in this era when the Romans, not understanding the ways of the Israelites, called them Christians, and this is how the black faces disappeared from Egypt. I am sure during the gulf war a lot of people were amazed to see so many black middle-eastern faces on their television screens. Some people were told before the crisis, that there were no black people in that region. Two good things that the war has done. One; showing that part of the world inhabited by black people, and two; showing the climatic conditions, whereby confirming the lie that there was no snow, or cold climate in that part of the world. This knowledge brought some light to the myth and confirm the fact that Jesus was not born in December, because of the cold the Romans did not collect taxes at this time, Mary did not ride a donkey, and shepherds could not graze their flocks. I wonder how these so-called teachers of Christianity would now explain the birth of Jesus on the 25th of December. How would the shepherds graze their flocks? How would poor Mary and a new baby travel on a donkey in the middle of winter? Thank God there are no dumb dogs in Israel to believe these vicious lies. We built the region and we still reside in it even though we are fewer now, our blood runs in the veins of the land.

THE FACE OF ISRAEL

Israel can be described as mysterious or mystical.

Before 1948 it was ruled by black kings. The first king being a Benjamite, Saul, unlike the most popular ones like David and Solomon who were Jews. The infighting was so terrible in the land that the tribes formed themselves into various kingdoms. Then gradually they scattered and merged into various cultures in Africa, especially those of North Africa like Libya, Yemen and on to the Iberian Peninsula of Portugal, Spain, eventually to Italy and even as far as southern France. They travelled as Jews. Some of them adopted the religion of Islam and travelled as Muslim conquerors. Then after losing power and being expelled from the area of the peninsula most of them went to Western Africa. They settled in places like the Gold Coast, the Mauritanian Empire,

Ivory Coast, Nigeria, Mali, etc. It was from these countries that they were sold as slaves to white Christians by Muslims.

Long before that ninety percent of the Jews remained in the land that was over run, conquered, or captured by the Assyrians, Babylonians, then the Romans, the Arabs, the Christian Crusaders, then the Turks and finally the British. Now you can see why a white Israel can capitalize on black history.

This is the mystery of it all. Hoping that eyes would be opened and ears expanded I sincerely hope that The Forgotten Israelites will practise the old saying, "Me and my brother against my cousin and me and my cousin against my enemies." As it is now, it's me and my cousin stake out my brother, while me and my enemies kill him.

Remember the bible is not a one page document. It does not say only love God and close. You must know your God and when you get to know Him, follow the instructions on how to serve Him. First you must find yourself. Remember when you look at the Libyans, the Saudies, the Egyptians, the Ethiopians, the Syrians and the others of the region you definitely would find them different from the Israelis today.

With all of the confusion of today's religions, there can only be one truth and when you find that truth, it will be your key to happiness. Christianity has taught you to love the world, which is wrong. Other religions have taught you to hate the white man. Both have failed. You should learn how to direct your love and to whom. Love your God and your family, then love your neighbour as yourself. You have thrown away the real God for a false god. He is now left without a people, and as He had said, that the Gentiles that believed on the God of Abraham, the God of Isaac and the God of Jacob would be welcome.

Acts 15:14 "Simeon hath declared how God at the first did visit the Gentiles, to take out of them a people for his name." (If they do the things God said for them to do.) Verse 20 "But that we write unto them, that they abstain from pollutions of idols, and from fornication, and from things strangled, and from blood."

So the time you take to hate, learn about your God, then teach others about Him.

Hebrew 5:12 "For when for the time ye ought to be teachers, ye have need that one teach you again which be the first principles of the oracles of God; and are become such as have need of milk, and not of strong meat."

52

The bible is a book for the children of slaves. It is not a Christian book. Yet the children of slaves who are the children of Jacob (Israel) allow people of other cultures to teach them.

There are only three places in the scriptures where the word "Christian" can be found, and only one came out of the mouth of an Israelite. I Peter 4:16 "Yet if any man suffer as a Christian, let him not be ashamed; but let him glorify God on this behalf."
This scripture explains the situation that Peter and his brethren found themselves in. Peter is preparing his brethren for battle with the enemy, in a court of law. In that court of law, they were tried as Christians, not Israelites. VERSE 12 "Beloved, think it not strange concerning the fiery TRIAL WHICH IS TO TRY YOU, as though some strange thing happened unto you."
In verse three he describes the enemy as Gentiles.
Could you have done anything about it in the seventeenth century, if they tried you as a NIGGER?

In Acts 11:26 it was the Romans again who called the Israelites Christians. "And when he had found him, he brought him unto Antioch. And it came to pass, that a whole year they assembled themselves with the church, and taught much people. And THE DISCIPLES WERE CALLED CHRISTIANS first in Antioch."

Acts 26:28 "Then Agrippa said unto Paul, Almost thou persuadest me to be a Christian."

The word Christian then, was almost as name-calling. They were in total darkness concerning spiritual things. These are the ways the word Christian was being used on Israelites. There is nothing that the Christian churches do today that is written in the bible. They do not follow any instruction. They created a new god with new ways. There was a reason for the name change by the white Romans. First, the name, then the culture and while we're at it, let's change the whole thing.

Open your eyes. Don't be fooled by the glitter of their brass. It is not pure. The bride in Christianity is the Great Whore, (See Revelations) not a maiden. Children of slaves, you are not a Muslim. You are not an Edomite. You are not a Christian. You are God's chosen people. You are the children of Israel.

THE FAMILY TREE

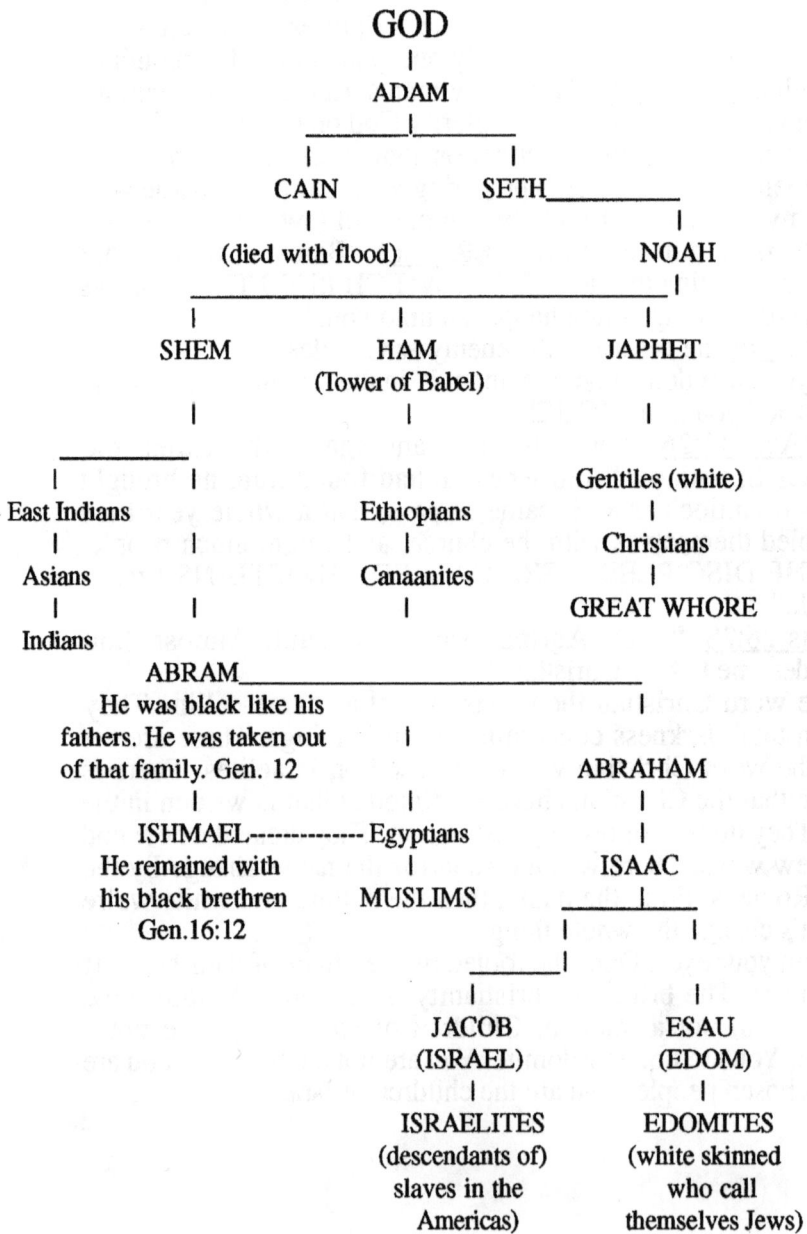

```
                        GOD
                         |
                       ADAM
         _____|_____
        |                                 |
       CAIN                             SETH_____
        |                                            |
  (died with flood)                               NOAH
   _____     |
  |                      |                       |
SHEM                    HAM                    JAPHET
                   (Tower of Babel)
  |                      |                        |
  _____
  |          |           |              Gentiles (white)
East Indians           Ethiopians              |
  |          |           |                  Christians
Asians                 Canaanites              |
  |          |           |              GREAT WHORE
Indians
           ABRAM_____
           He was black like his
           fathers. He was taken out          |
           of that family. Gen. 12        ABRAHAM
              |                                |
           ISHMAEL-------------- Egyptians     |
           He remained with         |        ISAAC
           his black brethren     MUSLIMS      |_____
           Gen.16:12                          |      |
                              _____|
                             |                |
                           JACOB            ESAU
                          (ISRAEL)         (EDOM)
                             |                |
                         ISRAELITES        EDOMITES
                        (descendants of)  (white skinned
                          slaves in the      who call
                           Americas)     themselves Jews)
```

ALL YOU NEED TO KNOW ABOUT SAINTS

Wars are not only fought with guns alone, even though they are the main weapon of war. There is another side of war. The propaganda machinery. This machinery, when correctly used, sometime is even more effective than the guns of war. There is evidence of this on every battle front including the gulf war.

Propaganda is used at various levels in the school system, on television, radio, almost in every aspect of life; and one of the most effective ways to penetrate spongy minds is to dress that lie with the clothing of truth.

Let's take religion for example. When last have you seen a picture of Mohamed and Kadijah? The real Queen of Sheba? Augustine? The pictures of these people would be rough sketches, poorly identified, or in some cases bright, but all white. Movies would put Charlton Heston as Moses and Yul Bryner as Pharaoh, even though some of these movie makers know that these characters were black. These images cling to your thoughts when you leave the cinema. You wonder how a white Samson could have what is known today as dread locks, but nevertheless Victor Mature played it brilliantly. You never realize that this also is a most effective way to utilize the propaganda machinery. Have you ever wondered why movie makers always look for the closest resembling actors to portray the real character and yet found a white woman to be the Queen of Sheba?

Let me tell you. She was great, so in your mind she should be white. What is really funny is that everyone believes, even the black teacher of the gospel, standing tall in his pulpit, looking good while Lucifer hangs over his head, or should I say the representative of Lucifer. The picture of a pagan whom they called Jesus. While he is pounding his fist and invoking your emotion and telling you of the Christians of old. What Christians? Then he will ask the congregation to pray, just as his white masters had taught him. All this is the machinery at work. This man no longer teaches you to be a teacher, he is still helping you to remain a slave. The Blackman needs to know how effective he can be.

If he doesn't buy in a store, he can close it down. If he doesn't ride the bus, he can put it off the road, if he doesn't go to the movies there'll be no Hollywood. If he turns to his God, there will be massive unemployment, especially in the institutes of the

55

correctional services. It is no propaganda that the United States cannot function properly without poverty, and black people provide the system with this raw material. Black people are the ones that make life easy for the rich. First, they gobble down the lies, then they follow the instructions to the very detail, allowing the system to rest easy and relax, while they remain the biggest spenders per capita.

Constantine and Pope Julius were the smartest of their time, because long after they were gone their images are still left implanted in the minds of their dependents. The philosophy of these two men was the most effective propaganda to black minds. It was not intentional on their part to keep black people in mental slavery. Their intention was to make everything good ROMAN, and by doing that everything turned out white, so their admirers and political puppies never bothered to change it. If it worked for them, by golly it's gonna work for us. So now we have Saint Patrick. Who is he? Saint George, Saint Helen etc. Can somebody tell me who in God's name are these people?

SAINTS are supposed to be the chosen of God, doing His bidding as messengers before and after they have passed from this world to paradise. After they have taken their proper place in the spiritual arena on the side of the Most High God; The God of Abraham, the God of Isaac and the God of Jacob.

All saints are Israelites, or spirits of Israelites. The saints are mentioned in the Holy Bible as God's people and so are the Israelites. Man cannot, I repeat, cannot know who will be or is a saint. For man to know who is a saint, it will mean that this man is playing God.

Now all of the prophets written about in the bible were Israelites. None of them were pagans or Gentiles, all of them were chosen by God in the spirit to do His work. These known men would be saints in our minds because their flesh had worked for God while they walked the earth, so will their spirits. Others that were not known but still remained dedicated Israelites who were not blessed with vibrant speech and powerful personalities, but nonetheless quietly and secretly served the Creator after the journey over the river in the spiritual Garden of Eden. These men unknown to the living, chosen by God, not known to man, would be saints also.

If man gave himself the authority to name saints and it is not propaganda , why then isn't Malcolm Little a saint (Malcolm X)?

56

Marcus Garvey? Martin Luther King Jr, etc.? There is proof that these men were born Israelites. There is more proof that they were Israelites, than any white philosopher can otherwise prove. There is no proof anywhere, apart from the propaganda, the lies, the misconception of a white philosophy working overtime to push down the throat of your mind, that their lies are the truth. There is not one single white prophet found anywhere in the Holy Bible.

Note when you see a picture of a white David, how new and perfect it is. A white Moses, white Jesus, white Solomon, the twelve bearded white men in your picture frame that hangs over your dinner table. Notice how recognizable they are. You can't miss the blonde or red head. Never kinky, never like wool, never red eyes or brown, always piercing green or blue eyes in close up. So why wouldn't you believe some man in Rome telling you about Saint Anthony. Who is he? Oh you don't care. Why should you? Everything white is right!

Let's now talk about spirits and relationship with them. Let's talk about how they affect you. The spirit is a dimension within man, the other two are soul and the visible one is body or flesh. Your body is the holding area for both soul and spirit. These three dimensions are the composition of man. Since we are not dealing with soul in this chapter, we would just be brief to prove that soul and spirit are within the body.

I Thessalonians 5:23 "And the very God of peace sanctify you wholly; and I pray God your whole spirit and soul and body be preserved blameless unto the coming of our Lord Jesus Christ."

Now let's turn again to the discussion of your relationship with your own spirit, or spirits in general. This topic is one that most North Americans cannot understand, but most of man's life and the things he does, or feels has to do with spirits.

One of the most important facts is the decline of black people today. Some are aware of the strength of their spirituality, but have no knowledge of how to use it properly. Others are just plain ignorant of this subject, caught up in a North American society, drifting with the flow of others. The former would know of his spiritual self, but most likely would turn to familiar spirits for help. The latter would go to a psychiatrist.

For a start, man must be aware of the knowledge of spiritual consciousness. Everyone undergoes some spiritual experience at least twice in their life. The first time is at birth, and by the time you begin to talk, your memory does not allow you to go that far back. For no one alive today can take his or her memory to the time of this mysterious journey from mama's womb to mama's hand. The other time is at death. By the time you realize it, you are on your way to the other side. That leaves the time between birth and death.

Not so long ago, your parents or grandparents passed on. Today it is different. Not so long ago, people were aware of the closing chapter in their lives. They would call their loved ones to their bed side and tell their most inner secrets, or give their blessing, then they would die, or they would scream, shout, or talk about the things facing them at the end of their journey through life. Some would even say things that you could not understand.

It is not that these things do not happen anymore, they do, but the awareness is no longer there. This is the natural journey of the dimensions. Today one will notice the reduction of this awareness. People are born, they live, they die with no awareness whatsoever of this process. The last public person that we all knew, a Forgotten Israelite, was such a strong Christian that if he had known I am sure he would have been teaching about it, but the ignorance of the Israelites today was prophesied in the bible.

Isaiah 1:2:3 "Hear, O heavens, and give ear, O earth: for the Lord hath spoken, I have nourished and brought up children, and they have rebelled against me. The ox knoweth his owner, and the ass his master's crib: but Israel doth not know, my people doth not consider."

Today's Israel is just like the Israel of old. This was Dr. Martin Luther King's speech before his death.

"We've got some difficult days ahead," he said. "But it really doesn't matter with me now. Because I've been to the mountaintop. I won't mind. Like anybody, I would like to live a long life. Longevity has its place. But I'm not concerned about that now. I just want to do God's will. And He's allowed me to go up to the mountain. And I've looked over, and I've seen the Promised Land. I may not get there with you, but I want you to know tonight that WE AS A PEOPLE will get to the Promised Land. So I'm happy tonight. I'm not fearing any man. Mine eyes have seen the glory of the coming of the Lord!"

One must look carefully at the well placed words Dr. Martin Luther King Jr. used before his death. After this spiritual revolution in the 1960's, the downhill path began.

Allow me to explain some things to you. Most people today are providing a home for adopted spirits. An adopted spirit is one who shares your body along with your own spirit and in most cases when your spirit is weak it takes over your body. These adopted spirits in most cases had bodies before and are living their lives all over again in yours. We can just imagine the deterioration of our lives through the recycling of spirits which are evil. We watch moral values slip away in the 60's, complete rebellion against authority, along with a new way of thinking in the 70's etc. To look at life in a very physical way would be to look at the recycling of a generation that is not worthy to be called God's children. The opportunity had presented itself in the sixties for black people to return to their God, but they refused to acknowledge the signs. It is amazing to note that with all the spiritual knowledge and self awareness thrown around in the sixties that today black people should be worse off in terms of their spirituality. The value of yesteryear's spiritual life is no more.

These Forgotten Israelites would always suffer because of this spiritual recycling. It was the fathers of these children that went into slavery in Egypt for their disobedience. It was the fathers of these children that were left in the wilderness for forty years. It was the fathers of these children that went into captivity again because they heard not the voice of the Lord.

God had promised their fathers that He would not give them the sickness and diseases of the Egyptians if they would obey Him. They did not then, and still do not now .

Deuteronomy 7:14-15 "Thou shalt be blessed above all people: there shall not be male or female barren among you, or among your cattle.
And the Lord will take away from thee all SICKNESS, and will put none of the evil DISEASES of Egypt, which thou knowest, upon thee; but will lay them upon all them that hate thee."

DEUTERONOMY 28:58-61 "If thou wilt not observe to do all the words of this law that are written in this book, that thou mayest fear this glorious and fearful name, the Lord thy God;
Then the Lord will make thy PLAGUES wonderful, and the PLAGUES of thy seed, even great plagues, and of long continuance, and SORE SICKNESSES, and of long continuance.
Moreover he will bring up thee all the DISEASES of Egypt, which thou wast afraid of; and they shall cleave unto thee.
Also EVERY SICKNESS, and EVERY PLAGUE, which is not

written in the book of this law, them will the Lord bring upon thee, until thou be destroyed."

This scripture still stands today. These Forgotten Israelites eat everything that their God had told them not to eat. They do everything that their God had told them not to do. They drink wine in their Christian churches which is the worse thing to do. To drink wine at an altar and calling upon God is punishable, because He never told you to do that.

I Corinthians 11:25-30 "After the same manner also he took the cup, when he had supped, saying, This cup is the new testament in my blood: this do ye, as oft as ye drink it, in remembrance of me.

For as often as ye eat this bread, and drink this cup, ye do shew the Lord's death till he come.

Wherefore whosoever shall **eat this bread, and drink this cup of the Lord, unworthily,** shall be guilty of the body and blood of the Lord.

But let a man examine himself, and so let him eat of that bread, and drink of that cup.

For he that eateth and drinketh unworthily, eateth and drinketh damnation to himself, not discerning the Lord's body.

FOR THIS CAUSE MANY ARE WEAK AND SICKLY AMONG YOU, AND MANY SLEEP."

Exodus 23:24-25 "Thou shalt not bow down to their gods, nor serve them, nor do after their works; but thou shalt utterly overthrow them, and quite break down their images.

And ye shall serve the Lord your God, and He shall bless thy bread, and thy water; and I will take SICKNESS away from the midst of thee."

After reading these scriptures one wonders how can people be so blind, but it is because of the things the Christians have taught God's children. It is now almost impossible for them to turn away from such teachings, but when you read what God had promised their fathers before them, it really makes you wonder.

When you realize how influential this new spiritual Egypt (U.S.A.) has become to God's children you just want to throw your hands up and give in, but when you look at the damage, one will find it very difficult to do. Babies making babies, babies born with aids, diseases of every sort are upon this people yet they sleep. They still continue to break God's laws. All these new customs were never popular among God's people. They were among white Christians. Now the children of slavery are indulging in every evil to satisfy their sexual appetite, men sleeping with unclean women, men sleeping with men, etc.

Leviticus 20:18 "And if a man shall lie with a women having her sickness, and shall uncover her nakedness; he hath discovered her fountain, and she hath uncovered the fountain of her blood; and both of them shall be cut off from among their people".

All these laws the children of slaves have broken, yet they continue to seek political and physical solutions. There can be no physical solution to these spiritual problems. For every sickness of these people is being caused by spiritual means.

If one understands the laws of the spirit, then one must understand how to live by them. The spirits of jealousy, along with the spirits of whoredom and spirits of the non -ambitious are all dwelling within man today. Then these men would die and walk the earth again as earth bound spirits. They would take a body that is unclean and live their lives all over again, killing, stealing, living in prisons, hospitals or on the streets, wherever they feel most comfortable, or where ever they lived before.

One should take a trip to the lands of Carnival where the celebration of the spirits is done in dance. In black lands or in black culture they call it a celebration of the freeing of slaves, so the entire population feels committed to such memory. In Trinidad for instance, in the Caribbean, it is an obsession, a national cry. It's a time when people forget their differences and enter the streets with the rhythm of the drums, steel pan or Congo drums. This even allows one, especially a Blackwoman, to absorb through the rhythm of the drums, spirits of the celebrations. In most cases it is the spirit of African ancestors or lost Israelites known as familiar spirits. There are always strong sexual overtures, with an enormous spiritual energy colliding and embracing participants. Because of ignorance this old scenario is being by-passed. In Brazil it is no different, it is just the same. You can almost feel the hand from the other side reaching out with a strong African culture.

In a white society you will find a less spiritual presence. You would also find a toned down rhythm, hereby not encouraging to the spirits of the Forgotten Israelites. There is a crowded visitation of African spirits whenever there is such a celebration. They can even take hold of white people when they participate, and give

61

them, if even for that time only, the sense of movement and rhythm.

The spirits are happy when there is dance, so in turn they make you happy. Rhythm and spirit goes together like hand in glove. Good spirits or bad. For it is written in the scriptures about this significant force. David danced for the Lord. This dance was also in the spirit.

II Samuel 6:14-16 "And David danced before the Lord with all his might: and David was girded with a linen ephod.
So David and all the house of Israel brought up the ark of the Lord with shouting, and with the sound of the trumpet.
And as the ark of the Lord came into the city of David, Michal Saul's daughter looked through a window, and saw king David leaping and DANCING before the Lord; and she despised him in her heart."

Let us not be confused about dancing in the spirit, for dancing in the spirit or with the spirit does not necessarily mean that you are dancing for God. Spiritual forces are divided into two categories; good and evil. One must try to be knowledgeable of the paths of which they take in this life. Many people are confused in this area, and it is very easy to make a spiritual mistake.

Today dancing for the ancestors is more important that dancing for God. Here is an example of a situation in South America. Ethel is what you might call a decent young lady, middle class, well mannered with strong Christian principles. She is a Sunday school teacher. On this particular Sunday while Ethel was teaching Sunday school, sounds were coming from across the streets, sounds of drums and spiritual celebrations. According to Ethel's upbringing this sort of behaviour was lewd and ill mannered, ungodly and down right evil, but on this particular Sunday Ethel removed her underwear in front of her students and began to dance, like you wouldn't believe. Whether she was lying on the ground or standing, her waist was moving like an elastic snake. Her face took on a coldness, while the grunts that came from her throat scared the children, some started screaming at this unusual behaviour of their Sunday school teacher. When adults approached hoping that she would stop she beckoned them to join her on the church floor with panties around her forefinger twirling over her head, while her waist was saying you can have me, if you can catch me. Suddenly the drumming stopped across the streets.

Ethel stopped, breathed a sigh of relief through heavy breathing, then sat down. After she discovered that she was holding her underwear in her hand, she looked up in bewilderment then bowed her head and cried uncontrollably. This is only one such story of the relationship between spirits and drums (rhythm). In a natural situation this would not have been the behaviour of Ethel. As a matter of fact, according to Ethel's teaching as a Christian such behaviour is of the devil. I wonder how Ethel would be seeing herself after this through her Christian eyes.

One must be very careful again on which side one is dancing and ignorance would never help. The black person is very receptive, especially the Blackwoman, being the symbol of the earth makes her a prime target for this evil. Please note too that most of these celebrations are on God's Sabbath, for instance; Caribana in Toronto, and very rarely on the day of the Christian Sunday. This is like a direct confrontation with God's law. For instance; in Trinidad the carnival could be held on Passover, but everything stops on the Christian's celebration of Ash Wednesday.

The Invisible Being

The children of slaves should try to find a new spirit, a spirit of their God and turn back to His ways. Let's try these scriptures for confirmation. We are now going to Egypt, where spiritual education began. Listen to Pharaoh telling his servants about Joseph and his spirit. Genesis 41:38 "And Pharaoh said unto his servants, can we find such a one as this is, a man to whom the spirit of God is?"

All through those days people of God had knowledge, wisdom and understanding as in Exodus 31:2:3 "See, I have called by name Bezaleel the son of Uri, the son of Hur, of the tribe of Judah: And I have filled him with the spirit of God, in wisdom, and in understanding, and in knowledge, and in all manner of workship." Also in Exodus 35:31.

Because the spirits of your fathers can no longer dwell saintly with you, you are left at the mercies of the damned. Christianity has provided you with the means to do so and a ticket to hell.

For most situations that occur to the children of slaves are spiritual. A perfect example how this works in a general way, is when a baby is born a genius at mathematics without even going to school means that the child entertains the spirit of a mathematician that lived before. This is the same way one can be born with the spirit of sickness, for there are many. There are also spirits of disease, spirits of the damned, even spirits of jealously.

Numbers 5:11-14 "And the Lord spake unto Moses, saying, Speak unto the children of Israel, and say unto them, if any man's wife go aside, and commit a trespass against him,
and a man lie with her carnally, and it be hid from the eyes of her husband, and be kept close, and she be defiled, and there be no witness against her, neither she be taken with the manner;
and the SPIRIT OF JEALOUSY come upon him, and he be jealous of his wife, and she be defiled; or if the SPIRIT OF JEALOUSY came upon him, and he be jealous of his wife, and she be not defiled;"

These spirits, like the old days, are responsible for most domestic violence. Yet without this spirit you cannot find love. For even God said, that He is a jealous God, because He loves His children (the children of Israel).

If you have a spirit of jealousy then that spirit must be directed in love, but if your own spirit is weak you would have no control over that direction. That's why one must first seek the first spirit and that is the spirit of truth.

Psalm 31:5 "Into thine hand I commit thy spirit: thou hast redeemed me, O Lord God of truth."

John 14:16-17 "And I will pray the Father, and He shall give you another comforter, that He may abide with you forever:
Even the SPIRIT OF TRUTH: whom the world cannot receive, because it seeth him not, neither knoweth him; but ye know him; for he dwelleth with you, and shall be with you."

John 15:26 "But when the comforter is come, whom I will send unto you from the Father, even the SPIRIT OF TRUTH, which proceedeth from the Father, he shall testify of me."

John 16:13 "Howbeit when he, the SPIRIT OF TRUTH; is come, he will guide you into all truth; for he shall not speak of himself; but whatsoever he shall hear, that shall he speak; and he will shew you things to come."

After you have searched for the knowledge of God's truth and not for that of man, then you may seek the spirit of God and not those of uncleanliness as stated in Matthew 12:43 "When the UNCLEAN SPIRIT has gone out of man, he walketh through dry places, seeking rest, and findeth none."

For God's people, the Forgotten Israelites, move from church to church, from religion to religion, because within them there is not the spirit of counsel, but the spirit of whoredom as stated in Hosea 4:12 "My people ask counsel at their stocks, and their staff declareth unto them: for the SPIRIT OF WHOREDOMS hath caused them to err, and they have gone a whoring from under their God." Hosea 5:4 "They will not frame their doings to turn unto their God; for the SPIRIT OF WHOREDOMS is in the midst of them, and they have not known the Lord."

If you are not of the God of Israel then you are not with the Almighty God. That means that you are not pure, but wounded and twisted and no prayer coming from your lips would be heard, for God does not hear wounded spirits. Proverbs 18:14 "The spirit of man will sustain his INFIRMITY: but a WOUNDED SPIRIT, WHO CAN BEAR?" Again you would see in Isaiah 19:14 "The Lord hath mingled a PERVERSE SPIRIT in the midst thereof: and they have caused Egypt to err in every work thereof, as a drunken man staggereth in his vomit."

With all these various spirits one must be wise enough to avoid those that can't help you to be progressive, constructive and economically strong. The Forgotten Israelites should seek the spirit of truth, the spirit of wisdom as stated in Isaiah 11:2 "And the spirit of the Lord shall rest upon him, THE SPIRIT OF WISDOM, and UNDERSTANDING, THE SPIRIT OF COUNSEL AND MIGHT, the SPIRIT OF KNOWLEDGE and of the fear of the Lord."

We have dealt with spirits of sickness and spirits of health, spirits of weakness and spirits of strength. It should not be difficult for the Forgotten Israelites to understand. Or is it? Remember spirits do pass through the time span from one time unto the next. Old spirits take new bodies and in some cases old spirits take another old body.

Matthew 17:3-4 "And, behold, there appeared unto them Moses and Elias talking with him. Then answered Peter, and said unto Jesus, Lord, it is good for us to be here: if thou wilt, let us make here three tabernacles, one for thee, and one for Moses and one for Elias."

Please do not forget that Elias and Moses were already dead in the days of Jesus and His disciples.

You know I am so afraid for my white brethren who know this truth and who serve the God of my Fathers. For their innocence would be on the guilty list of the fanatical black person who is being led in the other direction of hatred towards all white people, yet they will not even attempt to stop the destructive wheel of this most damaging propaganda.

Rather than making this a black and white issue, make it an issue of wrong and right, truth and lies. For this is the only way it can affect the system by having everybody on your side. There are lots of good white people out there who wouldn't care who or what God looks like, all they want to know is the truth about God. And don't forget it was the Romans who were the enemies of God's people, white Romans, yet it was a Roman who showed more love for God than the Israelites.

Matthew 8:8-12 "The centurion answered and said, Lord, I am not worthy that thou shouldest come under my roof: but speak the word only, and my servant shall be healed.
For I am a man under authority, having soldiers under me: and I say to this man, Go, and he goeth: and to another, Come, and he cometh; and to my servant, Do this, and he doeth it.
When Jesus heard it, he marvelled, and said to them that followed, Verily I say unto you, I have not found so great faith, NO, NOT IN ISRAEL.
And I say unto you, that many shall come from the east and west, and shall sit down with Abraham, and Isaac, and Jacob, in the kingdom of heaven.
But the children of the kingdom shall be cast out into outer darkness: there shall be weeping and gnashing of teeth."

This scripture provided us with a touch of history, philosophy, prophesy and awareness. What happened? It was a Roman who showed faith, acknowledged by Jesus, who told the gathering that the real children of Israel would be left out in the cold, because while others are seeking the true and living God, the real Israelites are clutching at straws.

The three saints or patriarchs are the foundation of Israel, and it is from these three that the government of the Almighty Abba would be based to do battle with the enemy at the time of Armageddon. Twelve thousand from every tribe of Israel. One hundred and forty four thousand would be sealed, (NO CHRISTIANS ALLOWED) which means that the 144,000 Israelites would not be judged a second time. They will act as policemen during the trials of Judgment Day. They will sit in judgment of the world. The Lord will judge the children of Israel, but the saints who are from the children of Israel will judge the

66

world.

Revelations 7:4 "And I heard the number of them which were sealed: and there were sealed an hundred and forty and four thousand of all the tribes of the children of Israel." See Revelations 14:3-4.

Since this scripture is so clear, one has to be really brainwashed not to understand what it's really saying, and what it is really saying, is that no man-god sitting down in Rome can know who is a saint. He himself is a pagan and a whore. How can he represent God?

Let's search the scriptures to find the real source of the saints. From the very beginning God said He had a government, of which He is head. He was betrayed by His deputy, so He cast him down to earth.

Let's now find out about who remained, but before we go into the scriptures, let me try to explain a few things to you.

(1 It is man who dies that becomes a saint. Not every man can be ordained to this office. (Israelites only).

(2 When a spirit is known to you through a past relationship such as grand mother, etc. such is a familiar spirit.

(3 Known spirits can help you, in dreams, visions, etc. but must not be used in any form of worship. Do not call upon them, invoke or otherwise.

(4 Spirits that were not known by you in the flesh but make themselves known to you afterwards are earthbound. Many of these spirits sometimes live together in one body. Western terms are "Multi-Personalities." These spirits do live their lives all over again within your body, once your own spirit is weakened. They allow you to carry out their orders and biddings. Sometimes they can be very criminal. In this category you'll find homosexuality rampant, even among priests. This is caused by having female entities possessing their bodies while the entities are still sexually active. The man then takes on the role of a woman in this sexual activity.

(5 Spirits that are not known to you in the flesh and cannot retain a physical body appearance always call for, or request things or substances, that are against the principles of the commandments of God. Example: They call for blood in most cases, the invoking of the dead, child molestation, etc. Such are demons or devils.

(6 Spirits that appear in the form of animals are also demons

67

and devils.

(7 A messenger or saint rarely identifies himself and never appears like an animal such as dogs or snakes. They always appear at the height of your cleanliness, deliver the message and never stick around for praise.

You can apply number two and three to VOODOO which means the worshipping of ancestors. This is common among Indians too, but not to the extent of voodoo. In this it is the minor partner.

Number four is the most popular in the established Christian churches. Numbers two, three and four are the deceivers that pinpoint number five and six as devils, and this in itself is a misconception.

Here is a typical example concerning the ways of the Catholic Church and the Black spiritual church. The Catholic Church retains the services of their priests even after death. The spirit of that dead priest is called upon to assist the one who is performing the exorcism. NOT GOD. You will notice that they call upon all these so-called saints, but what you are really noticing, are these men of the cloth, as they are known calling upon the dead.

The voodoo priest would call directly on the ancestors, not try to fool you, or cover up their dirt with the clothing of deception, as do the Catholics. Among the reasons noted, is the one that stands out. Almost every person that attends the black-spiritual church has some idea of what's going on. While in the Catholic church the ignorance in the congregation is overwhelming. The next time when your relative who happens to be a priest in the Catholic Church dies, you should ask the authority of the church for the body, to bury it yourself, and see how far you'll get.

The same way you cannot retain the body of a relative from a reputable lodge, it's the very same way you cannot obtain it from the Catholic Church, if that relative was a priest.

The spirit of the priest is needed and needed badly, especially if he was a good priest. This aspect of worship needs to be understood very clearly, for the bible speaks of familiar spirits in the following scriptures.

Leviticus 19:31 "Regard not them that have familiar spirits, neither seek after wizards, to be defiled by them: I am the Lord your God."

Unlike what the Christians might want you to believe, this law is not for the world. This law was and still is for the children of

Israel.

Leviticus 20:6 "And the soul that turneth after such as have familiar spirits, and after wizards, to go a whoring after them, I will even set my face against that soul, and will cut him off from among his people."

To have these familiar spirits could be of great risk to some men, including priests, for it is through this process that most men become homosexuals. This occurs when they entertain the spirits of women who continue to be sexually active in a male body. You will also notice the part that sex plays in such religious organizations led by a homosexual. Most homosexuals when known by their congregation always seek a way out, and one of the most popular scripture used is the story of Jonathan and David in I Samuel 18:1 "And it came to pass, when he had made an end of speaking unto Saul, that the soul of Jonathan was knit with the soul of David, and Jonathan loved him as his own soul"

One must read this entire chapter to feel that love expressed between two men. This is a love of mingled hearts not mingled bodies, so your priest is a liar and his mind is in the gutter, he is low down. This was the same kind of love that Jesus had for Peter.

Another point to note. The conventional Christian churches teach that it is a sin to practice or perform anything spiritual. For example, the burning of incense. They claim that this is wrong. This is simply because they do not understand. It is not the burning of the incense, but who you call upon. The god that you serve makes the difference. If there are images of false gods in every area of your church, then you cannot be burning incense to the God of Abraham, the God of Isaac and the God of Israel. If you entertain these white images, you cannot call upon a black God. If you entertain black demons, you can't call on the true God. If you entertain earthbound spirits, like most churches do, how can you be affected by the God of Israel.

If you serve the God of Israel, keep the Passover (not monthly communion), Day of Atonement, celebrate His New Year in the month of Abib (Nisan), don't drink wine at His altar in your church, don't pray the way as do the pagans, love your brother, your family, and your neighbour, let the God of Israel be the supreme of your life and not the Christian church; then you can safely say the smoke from your incense pot will be rising to the nostrils of the true and living God.

69

Here is an example for you to think about. Korah was an Israelite, just like Moses, but he showed no respect for leadership, only love of self, and this selfish attitude and disrespect for the authority of God's chosen, provides us with a perfect example. Now Korah and his friends that are mentioned in Numbers 16 rose up against Moses, claiming that they too were Israelites, encouraging others not to listen to Moses. Read Numbers 16:3-7 "And they gathered themselves together against Moses and against Aaron, and said unto them, Ye take too much upon you, seeing all the congregation are holy, everyone of them, and the Lord is among them: wherefore then lift ye up yourself above the congregation of the Lord?

And when Moses heard it, he fell upon his face: (Note he did not kneel down, clasp his hands and close his eyes).

And he spake unto Korah and to all his company, saying, Even tomorrow the Lord will shew who are his, and who is holy; and will cause him to come near unto him: even him whom he hath chosen will he cause to come near unto him. This do; Take you censers, Korah, and all his company;

And put fire therein, and put INCENSE in them before the Lord, to morrow: and it shall be that the man whom the Lord doth choose, he shall be holy: Ye take too much upon you, ye sons of Levi."

If you read this entire chapter you will get the full story, but we can read what happened to Korah through the burning of incense, even though it was done in the right way. We will prove that the same spiritual things used for God can be used for other spiritual purposes and not necessarily for God, THE GOD OF ISRAEL.

Let's turn now to verse 32-35 "And the earth opened her mouth, and swallowed them up, and their houses and all the men that appertained unto Korah, and all their goods.

They, and all that appertained to them, went down alive into the pit, and the earth closed upon them: and they perished from among the congregation.

And all Israel that were round about them fled at the cry of them: for they said, Lest the earth swallow us up also.

And there came out a fire from the Lord, and consumed the two hundred and fifty men that offered incense."

Now when Christians and others that do not understand, read the last verse, they shake their heads in confusion, telling you it's

not right. The question is not right or wrong, but who burned the incense. Let's read Exodus 30:8 "And when Aaron lighteth the lamps at even, he shall burn incense upon it, a perpetual incense before the LORD throughout your generations."
Exodus 40:5 "And thou shalt set the altar of gold for the incense before the ark of the testimony, and put the hanging of the door to the tabernacle."

Here is another example of the don'ts. Read Leviticus 10:1 "And Nadab and Abihu, the sons of Aaron, took either of them his censer, and put fire therein, and put incense thereon, and offered STRANGE fire before the Lord, which he commanded them NOT." Let's now read the second verse to find out the result of this disobedience. "And there went out fire from the Lord, and devoured them, and they died before the Lord."

Remember the Lord never said don't burn incense but one must know how and to whom you serve. Deuteronomy 33:10 "They shall teach Jacob thy judgments, and Israel thy law: they shall put incense before thee, and whole burnt sacrifice upon thine altar."

Turn to Jeremiah 44:17 which says that the practice of burning incense to the Queen of Heaven is wrong and yet this is a Roman Catholic tradition, the mother of all Christian churches.

We have dealt with familiar spirits and the practices of these churches that fool today's Israelites about incense and whether it may, or may not be used. Let me try to sum up before your very eyes through the scriptures, what must be known in order for you to be able to enjoy a fruitful spiritual understanding of self and your spirituality, as a child of slavery and a true Israelite.

Now as far-reaching as it may seem, God is not always with you! It is His saints, angels, messengers, or whatever you choose to call them. They are the ones that helped God's people through biblical history. This is the way it had always been. Not what your Sunday school teacher or others have been teaching you, that God is always with you. They are liars, or don't know anything at all. Unless God personally comes down from the heavens and by some act of reverence, communicate with you the individual the way he did with our father Moses, then it is His saints, angels, or spirits that visit.

Sorry Christians and others, but this is the truth. God visits man through the spirit. He is not always with man, instead, it is His saints. When this statement is being made in the scriptures,

71

you should take a close look at the events and situations.

Genesis 50:24-25 "And Joseph said unto his brethren, I die: and God will surely VISIT you, and bring you out of this land unto the land which He sware to Abraham, to Isaac and to Jacob. And Joseph took an oath of the children of Israel, saying, God will surely VISIT you, and ye shall carry up my bones from hence."

Jeremiah 5:9 "Shall I not VISIT for these things? saith the Lord: and shall not my soul be avenged on such a nation as this? Also Verse 29, Jeremiah 9: 9 and Jeremiah 27:22 "They shall be carried to Babylon, and there shall they be until the day that I VISIT them, saith the Lord; Then will I bring them up, and restore them to this place."

So far we have noticed that the Lord is going to visit His people. This means that He is not with them. Genesis 6:3 "And the Lord said, My spirit shall not always strive with man, for that he also is flesh: yet his days shall be an hundred and twenty years."

It is always a pleasure to deliver the truth that was hidden from man for generations. For as God is in heaven He will surely come down, if you call out to Him, or He will send His saints. Is this true?

When Moses asked God for help in Numbers 11:11 "And Moses said unto the Lord, Wherefore hast thou afflicted thy servant? and wherefore have I not found favour in thy sight, that thou layest the burden of all this people upon me?" this was God's reply. Read verse 17. "AND I WILL COME DOWN and talk with thee there: and I will take of the spirit which is upon thee, and will put it upon them; and they shall bear the burden of the people with thee, that thou bear it not thyself alone."

Now this was Moses, one of the greatest of all prophets and God had to come down to work with him, then how can your parson say to you that God is always with you?

Again let me explain that it is the angels that dwell in heaven that visit and saints that are in paradise. Genesis 22:11 " AND THE ANGEL OF THE LORD CALLED UNTO HIM OUT OF HEAVEN, and said, Abraham, Abraham: and he said. Here am I."

We have dealt with God separating Himself from man and coming down to visit man. We have also dealt with spirits of God and familiar spirits, and the difference of the two. We have dealt with the importance of knowing to whom or what and why you

72

burn incense. We have dealt with the common practice of men calling upon the dead, and making the ignorant believe he is calling on God.

Now let's really look into the duties of the saints. Who are they and what is their purpose? Let's find out first who are the saints through the scriptures.

Deuteronomy 33:1-3 "And this is the blessing, wherewith Moses the man of God blessed the children of Israel before his death.

And he said, The Lord came from Sinai, and rose up from Seir unto them; He shined forth from Mount Paran, and **he came with ten thousands of saints:** from his right hand went a fiery law for them.

Yea, he loved the people; all his saints are in thy hand: and they sat down at thy feet; every one shall receive of thy words."

Let's evaluate the sayings of this very important scripture. First, it says the Lord came with ten thousands saints. Who were they? It says He wrote a firey law for them. Who did He write the laws for? **The Israelites!** Please note this was almost the end of the forty years that they spent in the wilderness, and God had said when the old generation died, then He would lead them over Jordan to the promised land. So by this time a lot of Israelites had already died. These were now saints of God, and God told the other Israelites that they too could use the saints (spirits) for it says in Verse 3 "All his saints are in thy hand." meaning to do whatsoever they wish because they are representatives of God.

Call upon Him and He will send His saints. Psalm 132:9-10 "Let thy priest be clothed with righteousness; and let thy saints shout for joy.

For thy servant David's sake turn not away the face of thine anointed."

Psalm 148:14 "He also exalteth the horn of his people, **the praise of all his saints; even of the CHILDREN OF ISRAEL,** a people near unto him. Praise ye the Lord."

Now we have seen in the scriptures that the saints are the children of Israel, and the children of Israel were black. Then tell me how come these men that know it all, do not have one single black saint for you? As I said before the Lord will judge His people, but His saints along with the 144,000 sealed Israelites will assist Him in judging the world. Deuteronomy 32:36 "For the Lord shall judge his people, and repent himself for his servants, when he seeth that their power is gone, and there is non shut up, or left." Ezekiel 33:20 "Yet ye say, The way of the Lord is not equal. O ye house of Israel, I will judge you everyone after his ways."

We are seeing all over the scriptures about the saints being children of Israel, men of yesterday, today and tomorrow. The following scriptures will describe the role of the saints in the Day of Judgment.

Daniel 7:27 "And the kingdom and dominion, and the greatness of the kingdom under the whole heaven, shall be given to the people of the saints of the Most High, whose kingdom is an everlasting kingdom, and all dominions shall serve and obey him."

Jude 14 "And Enoch also, the seventh from Adam, prophesied of these, saying, Behold, the Lord cometh with ten thousand of his saints."

Psalms 106:16. "They envied Moses also in the camp, and AARON THE SAINT of the Lord."

It is a shame that others not qualified to teach on this particular issue, are doing so, when the Forgotten Israelites should have been the ones teaching about it.

White women today, who live in the corridors of spiritual knowledge, only wish that they could somehow open the door and really see what is going on inside. They have everything at their disposal, for all the literature on palm reading, and things of that nature are written by white people, a people so desperate to experience the unseen. A black spiritualist wouldn't need any book, to them it comes natural.

There is a story about a woman in the land of make-belief (California), who claims to have an entity (spirit) that is 35,000 years old, yet this entity speaks fluent English through her. How dumb can people be? A spirit cannot be trained in changing old habits and culture. If you attain a spirit that is Chinese from China, then that spirit would speak and act Chinese, an African spirit would speak and act African, a hip-shorted person at the time of death, would walk hip-shorted as a spirit through a medium who is not hip-shorted. So tell me, how can a spirit of the old world appear, and speak English that they have never heard of in their lifetime? Let's call that spirit RAMTA. Now the name Ramta is either African, or Asian and 35,000 years ago there was no U.S.A. nor Britain. How can these spiritual ignoramuses explain to an intelligent person, that they have an African spirit

74

35,000 years old, now living (in their body) in the United States, and speaking perfect English? These are the lies that white people are circulating, and soaking in, because of that need to understand spiritual things. The knowledge of creation, spirits, and everything about them, astrology, and all forms of worship, the naming of the planets etc., were all originated from what is known today as Africa. All others who take it upon themselves, proclaiming authority on this matter, have no authority.

With this knowledge you should be aware of the difference between the righteous and the ungodly, the truth and the lie. Remember, there will always be the unseen every time you pray or burn incense, or do anything spiritual. So make sure that the unseen are angels or saints of the Lord our God, and not your grandmother or Benjie or somebody you use to know. You must know the difference between the light and the dark, the good and the evil. The choice is now yours.

Ask yourself why Jesus told Peter that Satan wants him and He (JESUS) was going to pray for him. Luke 22: 31-32 "And the Lord said, Simon Simon, behold, SATAN hath desired to have you that he may sift you as wheat.
But I have prayed for thee, that thy faith fail not and when thou art converted STRENGTHEN THY BRETHREN."

Think on it, think hard on it. Peter was Jesus' best friend. Let me remind you again that everything that was done was spiritually done. Today Christians teach you that you should just trust in GOD and everything will be alright. Not so my brother, not so my sister. It is the knowledge of your spirituality and how to use it, that would make all the difference in this world of ignorance in which we live.

W - O - M - A - N

She's my mother - My father's wife
She's the one who gave me life
She's my sister - she's my friend
A relationship that can never end
She's my daughter - Oh! She's my child
Who'll be a mother all over again

The symbol of creation - That's my wife
The strength of the other half of my life
She moulds the seed - Just like the land
She gave birth to every man

She's beautiful - She's precious
She's great and marvellous
Without her would mean
Without me
Without her there is no man
She's the source of all
She's W O M A N
She's woman

This chapter is dedicated to all women, but to the Blackwoman particularly, since she is the mother of all mankind. Have you ever wondered what it is about a woman that makes her do the things she does, or act the way she acts? Have you ever stopped to think why is it you sometimes hate her, but still can't help loving her?

The answer is simple, so simple that we take it for granted. She is the symbol of every aspect of life.

The earth is that source of life that brings forth our food, our very survival depends on the land. Maybe that's why it is often called MOTHER EARTH.

Let us look into this subject in greater depth. Every country that delivered up our forefathers is referred to as SHE, HER or MOTHER LAND. Every living thing upon this earth that is significant to life would not have been if it wasn't our Mother Earth. Yet one wonders if the woman is so powerful how then is she being dominated or mistreated by men?

Again the answer is simple. Ignorance of self. A man can never bare a child, since he cannot have the experience of the monthly cycle. Nor can a woman develop hair on her chest, or a beard on her face, or be as big and muscular as a man. The sooner we realize our biological differences the better our lives will be. From creation God had made the woman different from the man, and made them different from animals. Today men want to be women and women want to take the place of men. This is the first law that the human race has broken. Wanting to be something or someone they're not, thereby reducing the level of their ability to function properly.

History has shown us how great women were, especially Blackwomen. Today's Christians would like to paint those Blackwomen white. Blackwomen were rulers of nations, leaders in society and had taught the world many things. We would prove in this chapter that it was the white Christian male who had placed not only Blackwomen, but also their own, in positions of rebellion. Because of the suppression and oppression and fear. These men created laws that forced women to rebel. This fear arose after they thought that they had controlled the Africans and now right before their very eyes, the African spirits still lived in whom they identified as their own women.

Women that had a generation of African and Asian origins were then called witches. A perfect example, are the Gypsies. They were always called Europeans, when instead they are from a tribe of East-Indians, with their root in Africa.

It is very clear that the situation existing today started with the domination of the white man. He is so wrapped up in power that he could not see the hurt he was inflicting on his own women. His ignorance of spiritual things did not allow him to see the difference between one woman and the next. In his eyes there were two types of women. The one he used and the other that he could not. If the white man cannot understand something he destroys it and when he can understand it, he tries to control it.

77

Black Women in Leadership

The first woman that comes to mind is MAKEDA, who was the Queen of Sheba. Sheba as you well know was a vast area in Africa. This area was also called by other names from time to time, such as Cush, Seba or Saba. All these are the names of the children of Ham.

Genesis 10:6-7 "And the sons of Ham: CUSH, and Mizraim, and Phut, and Canaan.
And the sons of Cush: SEBA, and Havilah, and Sabtah, and Raamah, and Sabtecha: and the sons of Raamah: SHEBA and Dedan." Egypt was also called the land of Ham.
Psalms 105:23 "Israel also came into **Egypt**: and Jacob sojourned in the land of **Ham**." This confirms the bond between Egypt and Ethiopia.

Cush was another name given to this vast land of the Ethiopians. It was also called Abyssinia. Its people had ruled as far as Babylon (Chaldea) and Egypt. One can just imagine the might and power. In the height of all its glory Sheba was ruled by a woman. One must remember that the Ethiopia we know today came into being by Menelik II (1844-1913). Haile Selassie came on the scene in 1916. So we must be careful when we use symbols and colours believing they are from Ethiopia, and a direct gift to us. We must be sure which Ethiopia we're talking about, the old or the new. In the days between 1844 and now, a lot has been changed to suit the purpose of man.

Here's a little history on Makeda and the bond between Israel and Ethiopia. I Kings 10:1-10 "And when the queen of Sheba heard of the fame of Solomon concerning the name of the Lord, she came to prove him with hard questions.
And she came to Jerusalem with a very great train, with camels that bare spices, and very much gold, and precious stones: and when she was come to Solomon, she communed with him of all that was in her heart.
And Solomon told her all her questions: there was not anything hid from the king, which he told her not.
And when the Queen of Sheba had seen all Solomon's wisdom, and the house that he had built,
And the meat of his table, and the sitting of his servants, and the attendance of his ministers, and their apparel, and his cupbearers, and his ascent by which he went up unto the house of the Lord:

there was no more SPIRIT IN HER.

And she said to the king; It was a true report that I heard in mine own land of thy acts and of thy wisdom.

Howbeit I believed not the words, until I came, and my eyes had seen it: and, behold, the half was not told me: thy wisdom and prosperity exceedeth the fame which I heard.

Happy are thy men, happy are these thy servants, which stand continually before thee, and that hear thy wisdom.

Blessed be the Lord thy God which delighted in thee, to set thee on the throne of Israel: because THE LORD LOVED ISRAEL FOREVER, therefore made he thee king, to do judgment and justice.

And she gave the king an hundred and twenty talents of gold, and of spices very great store, and precious stones: there came no more such abundance of spices as these which the QUEEN OF SHEBA gave to king Solomon." This can also be found in II Chronicles 9.

The above is confirmation of the difference of worship between the Ethiopians and the Israelites. Note that the Queen of Sheba separates herself from the God of Israel, yet gave Him honour and identified His love for the children of Israel.

Makeda's mother was Queen Ismenie and in 1005 B.C. Makeda was made queen after the death of her father. She ruled Ethiopia for fifty years. The area that was called Sheba stretched from India to Upper Egypt, Syria, and Arabia. In other words it can be stated that the land known as Africa today, could have been the old Ethiopia. That is why all people in that area in the bible were called Ethiopians. You'll find the merchant's wealth of this great empire in Ezekiel 27:22-24. "The merchants of SHEBA and Raamah, they were thy merchants: they occupied in thy fairs with chief of all spices, and with all precious stones and gold. Haran, and Canneh, and Eden the merchants of SHEBA, Asshur, and Chilmad, were thy merchants.

These were the merchants in all sorts of things, in blue clothes, embroidered work, and in chests of rich apparel, bound with cords, and made of cedar, among thy merchandise."

Yet we hear today that women always had to take their place behind men. This is not the case in history about Blackwomen. They were always strong since the first black woman, Eve. The placement of women by Christians in today's society, makes them feel inferior.

If two things or two beings were created for different purposes, how then can one be inferior to the other? If they both stand on the same platform, then and only then can one be inferior. Christianity has placed women on that platform, parallel to men, hereby placing them in competition with each other. Further accusing them of crimes of nature, challenging them, hereby placing women in a corner of rebellion.

History has constantly proven that women were capable of holding their own providing they weren't trying to grow hair on their chest and becoming men. Women in the old days in Africa did not lose any of their femininity, because they were leaders in society. They took their role seriously and executed their mission. They still bore babies, still were romantic or in today's terms "sexy". If white men (Christians) had just left them alone they would not be in the arena of identification today. Telling a woman that her place is in the bedroom and the kitchen is like telling a man he has to sweat until he's dead. In most cases this might be the law of a tradition handed down from ancient times but neither men nor women want to be told.

There was Queen Judith, the Falasha queen as she was known, who ruled Ethiopia for forty years. She was not only a political figurehead, but known also for her military ability. This queen was a strong Israelite who hated the very name of Christianity. She conquered Axum and destroyed the Christians.

Egypt or Kemet also had great women as heads of government. One of them ruled at the end of the dynasty of Alexander the Great. Her name was Cleopatra. This queen had lost the features of her Macedonian ancestry. The first of which was Ptomely, a general in Alexander's army. At the time of her reign she was like any other Egyptian woman, black. Her mother was a Nubian.

Let's take a look at some very famous queens who were considered extremely beautiful. NEFERTARI. She was queen of Egypt, wife of Ahmose I, co-founder of the 18th dynasty of Egypt (around 1580 B.C.)

The mother of Amenhotep III, MUTEMUA believed in child education before birth. As a result it was noted that her son ruled Egypt from about 1420-1411 B.C.

History will never forget the story of ISIS, who was an Egyptian goddess that Christianity painted white, and called her Mary. She was the black Madonna that even the Pope of today recognizes. Her statue or picture is all over Europe. Even Cleopatra worshipped her in her day. Augustine praised her and installed her in the Catholic church. Since everything in that church had to be white she was no longer the Black Madonna, but painted by Michelangelo under the instructions of Pope Julius II WHITE. Nevertheless she was a woman. She was known as Lady of Heaven, Queen of Heaven, Lady of Light, Queen of Honey, Lady of the Sunrise, Mistress of Magic, etc. Historians believed that she originated from Ethiopia, but her popularity soared in Egypt and eventually around the world.

There is a story that Isis' husband Osiris, was like a god. His brother Seth killed him and she resurrected him from the dead. She then gave birth to their son, Horus. Osiris was known as king of the dead. Horus was later called Apollo or King of the living by the Romans.

Queen Dahia-al Kahina fought the Arabs in North Africa. She also was a known Israelite from the tribe of Simeon. She was killed in battle by a Muslim, Hassan-Ben-Numan in 705 A.D. trying to save Africa from the threat of Islam. Black women had been great inventors too. The whole fashion line of lipstick, colouring, hair management came from African women. That brings us to the second stage of this chapter. How did it all change.

THE SPIRITUAL ASPECT

History has provided us with information that the fanatics would not want to hear. First, we have read that Queen Judith, an Ethiopian, was trying to rid Africa of the menacing Christians. Then we read about Queen Dahia also trying to rid Africa of the threat of Islam. Both of these queens were Israelites. One was called a Falasha, and the other from the tribe of Simeon.

The power of worship that surrounded black people in B.C. and early A.D. that they had brought with them through the centuries threatened the white invaders. Most whites at that time longed for this sort of power which they heard of, but could not attain or understand.

The Egyptians and Ethiopians were the first to utilize the spirits in an organized way, calling upon them, honouring them as gods. These gods (spirits) were then transformed into visible objects such as birds, lion heads, man shaped beasts with more

81

than one head, and beasts with more than one pair of hands. These images were placed in temples in ancient Africa where men and women prayed. Some were taken to India, to Hindustan sometime after the rule of Makeda, queen of Sheba, or when Sheba was called Cush, ruled by one of its greatest kings ever, PIANKHI. Piankhi ruled both Egypt and Ethiopia from 750 B. C.

It was Piankhi's sister Amenirdas, who was known as a Cushite priestess or chief prophetess of Amon and queen of Thebes. This queen helped to spread the worshipping of the god with multiple hands and heads, sometimes in the shape of a lion, a bird, and sometimes even as a man. She prayed to these images in the temple of Nagaa. In those days the gods of the earth (spirits) were known to men of spiritual wisdom. It was for this kind of power, generated by this kind of worship, which enticed Alexander the Great to conquer Egypt in order to obtain the knowledge of the Grand Lodge. This is where most spiritualist of the day were educated. That is why Alexander took most of the information back to Greece and called on all those gods which were black spirits or the origin of a black spiritual force. All Greeks believed in the god Imhotep who was an Egyptian ruler, inventor, builder, statesman and a scholar. The Greeks called him a god.

If we notice very carefully we will find that the awareness of spirits and spiritual forces originated in Africa. It went to Asia, India in particular, Greece and eventually rested in the cradle of modern society, Rome. The spiritual practices of every day life were very common. The children of Israel depended on the knowledge of the spirits and so did the Egyptians. Even Moses, a cultured Egyptian was brought up with full spiritual knowledge. He was educated in the temple of the magicians as it was called then. All knowledge of the gods, in the old days was similar to the knowledge of the spirits, until the children of Israel went into Egypt. They taught the Egyptians about one God. Here is where the difference appeared. Without knowledge one can classify all spiritual practices as evil, forgetting a very important factor; that God is a spirit. John 4:24 "God is a Spirit: and they that worship him must worship him in **SPIRIT AND IN TRUTH.**"

If this is not recognized by the worshipper, then we become like worshippers of the last days of Roman Christianity, when no spiritual practices were allowed by Jews except the pagan practices of the Pope and the Emperors.

FEMININE INFLUENCE
& STRENGTH

It is so easy to bypass the strength and influence of a woman. We take it for granted because we have mothers, sisters, daughters, aunts, etc., so the strength is always with us, even though we never pay much attention to it. If one carries out the exercise of awareness, one will find that there is no cigarette smoke in the room, while one is in the room. The awareness of the cigarette smoke occurs when you leave and re-enter the room. That is why we should re-enter the room of our minds to discover the strength and influence of a woman.

Ever since the human race started, the influence was there as in the first woman, Eve. For Adam was a good man according to the scriptures. It was Eve who influenced Adam to have sex with her after she discovered the erotic sensation with Lucifer. With all of Adam's strength and faith he could not resist this woman. The scriptures also say for a woman, a man must leave his father and mother. Genesis 2:24 "Therefore shall a man leave his father and his mother, and shall cleave unto his wife: and they shall be one flesh."

Note also that the appeal by God and the prophets was always for the woman to lead their men folk in the right direction. It is proven time and time again, that even though men are biologically made up with enormous physical strength, it is the woman who carries the greatest strength of all, THE SPIRITUAL STRENGTH. It was the women of Israel that the prophet Jeremiah appealed to, to stop burning incense to the Queen of Heaven. It was the women who were leading the men folk in the wrong way.

Jeremiah 44:4-11 &15-21 "Howbeit I sent unto you all my servants the prophets, rising early and sending them, saying, Oh, do not this abominable thing that I hate.
But they harkened not, nor inclined their ear to turn from their wickedness, to burn no incense unto other gods.
Wherefore my fury and mine anger was poured forth, and was kindled in the cities of Judah and in the streets of Jerusalem: and they are wasted and desolate, as at this day.

83

Therefore now thus saith the Lord, the God of hosts, the God of Israel: Wherefore commit ye this great evil against your souls, to cut off from you man and woman, child and suckling, out of Judah, to leave you none to remain:

In that ye provoke me unto wrath with the works of your hands, burning incense unto other gods in the land of Egypt, whither ye be gone to dwell, that ye might cut yourselves off, and that ye might be a curse and a reproach among all the nations of the earth?

Have ye forgotten the wickedness of your fathers, and the wickedness of the kings of Judah and the wickedness of their WIVES, and your own wickedness, and the wickedness of your WIVES, which they have committed in the land of Judah, and in the streets of Jerusalem?

They are not humbled even unto this day, neither have they feared, nor walked in my law, nor in my statues, that I set before you and before your fathers.

Therefore thus saith the Lord of hosts, the God of Israel, Behold, I will set my face against you for evil, and to cut off all Judah."

Verse 15-17

"Then all the men which knew that their WIVES had burned incense unto other gods, and all the women that stood by, a great multitude, even all the people that dwelt in the land of Egypt, in Pathros, answered Jeremiah, saying,

As for the word that thou hast spoken unto us in the name of the Lord, we will not hearken unto thee.

But we will certainly do whatsoever thing goeth forth out of our own mouth, to burn incense unto the Queen of Heaven, and to pour out drink offering unto her as we have done, we, and our fathers, our kings, and our princes in the cities of Judah, and in the streets of Jerusalem: for then had we plenty of victuals, and were well, and saw no evil."

Note the role the women played. They were the ones that burned the incense to false gods (another woman - Queen of Heaven). They even baked cakes to their gods. Jeremiah 44:19 "And when we burned to the QUEEN OF HEAVEN, and poured out drink offerings unto her, did we make her cakes to worship her, and pour out drink offerings unto her, without our men?"

Let's take a look at Samson, who is another symbol of physical strength, but it was the woman who led him with her spiritual strength. Judges 14:1-3 "And Samson went down to Timnath, and saw a woman in Timnath of the daughters of the

84

Philistines.

And he came up, and told his father and his mother, and said, I have seen a woman in Timnath of the daughters of the Philistines: now therefore get her for me to wife.

Then his father and his mother said unto him, Is there never a woman among the daughters of thy brethren, or among all my people, that thou goest to take a wife of the uncircumcised Philistines? And Samson said unto his father, Get her for me: for she pleaseth me well."

In this case it was a spiritual arrangement with God. Let us read the fourth verse. "But his father and his mother know not that it was of the Lord, that he sought an occasion against the Philistines: for at that time the Philistines had dominion over Israel."

God knew that if He had to get him to do what he wanted him to do then he had to place a woman, even one from the enemy's camp, before him.

It was a similar situation again with Solomon. God was afraid that He would lose the loyalty of His favourite son to other gods through women. I Kings 11:1-2 "But king Solomon loved many strange women, together with the daughter of Pharaoh, women of the Moabites, Ammonites, Edomites, Zidonians, and Hittites;

Of the nations concerning which the Lord said unto the children of Israel, Ye shall not go in to them, neither shall they come in unto you: for surely they will TURN AWAY YOUR HEART AFTER THEIR GODS: Solomon clave unto these in love."

God was always worried that the freedom which He gave to His people would hurt Him. However being a Keeper of Covenants, He indulged in the warnings of the prophets to show His children the difference between good and evil and the path that they should take. Even Solomon's father, David, committed his sin through women also.

II Samuel 11:2-5 "And it came to pass in an eveningtide, that David arose from off his bed and walked upon the roof of the king's house: and from the roof he saw a woman washing herself; and the woman was very beautiful to look upon.

And David sent and inquired after the woman. And one said, Is not this Bathsheba, the daughter of Eliam, the wife of Uriah the Hittite?

And David sent messengers and took her; and she came in unto him, and he lay with her, for she was purified from her uncleanness; and she returned unto her house.

And the woman conceived, and sent and told David, and said, I am with child."

To see God's punishment unto David for what he had done read II Samuel 12:10-12. "Now therefore the sword shall never depart from thy house: because thou hast despised me, and hast taken the wife of Uriah the Hittite to be thy wife.

Thus saith the Lord, Behold, I will raise up evil against thee out of thine own house, and I will take thy wives before thine eyes, and give them unto thy neighbour and he shall lie with thy wives in the sight of this sun.

For thou didst it secretly, but I will do this things before all Israel, and before the sun."

That child died because God was not pleased with David for what he had done. It is proven in the scriptures when God wanted to punish His children for the worshipping of false gods it was the women He turned to first.

Lamentation 2:2-5 "The Lord hath swallowed up all the habitations of Jacob, and hath not pitied: he hath thrown down in his wrath the strong holds of the DAUGHTER OF JUDAH; he hath brought them down to the ground: he hath polluted the kingdom and the princes thereof.

He hath cut off in his fierce anger all the horn of Israel: he hath drawn back his right hand from before the enemy, and he burned against Jacob like a flaming fire, which devoureth round about.

He hath bent his bow like an enemy: he stood with his right hand as an adversary, and slew all that were pleasant to the eye in the tabernacle of the DAUGHTER OF ZION: he poured out his fury like fire.

The Lord was as an enemy: he hath swallowed up Israel, he hath swallowed up all her palaces: he hath destroyed his strong holds, and hath increased in the DAUGHTER OF JUDAH mourning and lamentation."

He also had pity for Israel when He looked at the women. Lamentations 2:10-13 "The elders of the DAUGHTER OF ZION sit upon the ground, and keep silence: they have cast up dust upon their heads; they have girded themselves with sackcloth: the VIRGINS OF JERUSALEM hang down their heads to the ground.

Mine eyes do fail with tears, my bowels are troubled, my liver is poured upon the earth, for the destruction of the DAUGHTER OF MY PEOPLE; because the children and the sucklings swoon in the streets of the city.

They say to their mothers, Where is corn and wine? when they swooned as the wounded in the streets of the city, when their soul was poured out into their MOTHERS' bosom.

What thing shall I take to witness for thee? what thing shall I liken to thee, O DAUGHTER OF JERUSALEM? what shall I equal to thee, that I may comfort thee, O VIRGIN DAUGHTER OF ZION for thy breach is great like the sea; who can heal thee?"

Again there is a powerful ability to lead, that is rested in the spiritual corner of a woman that we all take for granted. The wrath of God is seen here, as He described it through His prophets again and again, that it was the daughters of His people that led His people astray.

II Kings 19:21-22 "This is the word that the Lord hath spoken concerning him; THE VIRGIN THE DAUGHTER OF ZION hath despised thee, and laughed thee to scourn: THE DAUGHTER OF JERUSALEM hath shaken her head at thee.

Whom hast thou reproached and blasphemed? and against whom hast thou exalted thy voice, and lifted up thine eyes on high? even against the Holy One of Israel." Also in Isaiah 37:22-23.

One must note very carefully that most spiritual practitioners are women and most parishioners are women. To gain an increase in membership in political parties or other social organizations, you must satisfy the members, directly or indirectly. There must be lots of women activists. The same thing is applicable in the organized church, even clubs or party houses. The more women there are, the more likely is the chance of becoming a success.

Who did Saul visit to find out about himself? A woman, of course with a familiar spirit. I Samuel 28:7-13 "Then said Saul unto his servants, Seek me a WOMAN that hath a familiar spirit, that I may go to her, and inquire of her. And his servants said to him, Behold, there is a WOMAN that hath a familiar spirit at Endor.

And Saul disguised himself, and put on other raiment, and he went, and two men with him, and they came to the WOMAN by night: and he said, I pray thee, divine unto me by the familiar spirit, and bring me him up, whom I shall name unto thee.

And the woman said unto him, Behold, thou knowest what Saul hath done, how he hath cut off those that have familiar spirits, and the wizards out of the land: wherefore then layest thou a snare for my life, to cause me to die?

And Saul sware to her by the Lord, saying, As the Lord liveth there shall no punishment happen to thee for this thing.

Then said the woman, Whom shall I bring up unto thee? And he said, Bring me up Samuel.
And when the woman saw Samuel, she cried with a loud voice: and the woman spake to Saul, saying, Why hast thou deceived me? for thou art Saul.
And the king said unto her, Be not afraid: for what sawest thou? And the woman said unto Saul, I saw gods ascending out of the earth."

You should notice that women are symbolic of the earth, and the earth takes in seed and gives out fruit. The same with a woman. She is receptive of spirits and she gives out the fruit of that spirit, good or evil. In most cases she gives out the work of familiar spirits because of her receptiveness.

The woman of the Forgotten Tribes of Israel should be aware of her spiritual self. She is far freer now than she was after the abolition of slavery, but now she finds herself competing with other women and with other people. While she is busy competing in the material world her spiritual capability is slowly taking the back seat. It was this woman that taught the world things they knew nothing about concerning the spirits. It was the white Christian male that sought to re-educate the Israelite woman after he had tried so hard to eliminate her ancestors, along with the knowledge of their teachings, because of fear.

THE ERA OF WITCHES

In its original sense, the word witch is often misused and misunderstood by the Europeans. It is of African origin, whose practitioners are far more frightening in their practices than their European counterparts. It was said that the African slaves in the New World flew from plantation to plantation at night to satisfy their spiritual appetite. The former slaves known today as Jukas in Suriname were noted for this. In Guyana it was also believed that slaves flew away from their master's plantation and formed a village called Mocha-Canal. In Haiti, this was a common practice. It is believed that because of this spiritual richness the French government was so afraid to keep Toussaint L'Ouverture in prison in Haiti that they moved him to France, where he died in a French cell away from his own people in 1803. There is a slave version to Dracula where slaves used to fly, as well as suck the blood of both human and cattle. This kind of spiritual practice had to be handed down from generation to generation. While the Dracula version can be classified as a myth, there is evidence in the West Indies, even today, that these practices were real. In Guyana they were called Ole Higue.

From Africa to Asia, then to Europe, was the practice of what the Christian conceived to be witches, as is written in Exodus 22:18 "Thou shalt not suffer a witch to live."

The white version of witches started with the Gypsies, who are not white but rather an East Indian tribe that travelled from India through Turkey and made their way on to the Iberian Peninsula of Spain, Italy, Portugal and part of France, and into Eastern Europe. This was the beginning of the destruction of women, all women by white Christians. These Christians who taught others about spiritual things were always fearful of its hidden meaning, for they themselves knew nothing about it. They exercised such great authority, but their fear was real because of ignorance. Witches, according to the bible were evil so Christianity destroyed any and everything that appeared as such, thereby destroying about 9 million women between the 15th and 17th centuries, burning them at the stakes.

You can see that it was fear, because the same reason that caused the death of these 9 million women is being practiced today openly, not only in the Christian church, but also is the custom of the Christian society. Take Halloween for example. This evil practice pays homage to the Queen of the Night.This was a specific time to remember the ancestors and was not very different from Voodoo. Today the same Christians make Halloween a costume celebration for the children, or so they say. Women were burnt at the stake for this pagan custom, yet today the Forgotten Israelites participate fully in this evil. Halloween was known as the sabbath for the witches, also known as the black mass.

In 1484 Pope Innocent VIII (1432-1492) condemned witches because no one was paying attention to his Christianity and the Christian church. He ordered the baptizing of all babies. It was the white male against all women. It was unlawful even to carry out at that time, a very normal practice of giving birth with the help of the familiar old woman, that later on was called a midwife. This practice was a known art to the black women of slavery. They even delivered their master's babies. They mothered the new world, yet in certain parts of Europe the practice was outlawed. The old woman was replaced with a white male doctor who delivered the babies. All other forms of assisting mothers in birth were outlawed. Therefore, eventually rendering women incapable of even giving natural birth, something they have been doing since man was created by God. It was the woman who acted the part of God and naturally gave birth to the first generation after God's creation of man.

Women have led all the way. They have led through evil and good, through physical leadership and most common in the spiritual directions. Today a woman is still in the position of leadership, spiritual or otherwise, but is very ignorant of it.

Let's direct our attention to the women of the Lost Tribes of the Israelites. It is on their shoulders, the generation of the Forgotten Israelites will lean. It is these women that will have to start teaching their babies all over again. It is these women that will have to be the ones to denounce the evils of Christianity and lead their men folk and their sons and daughters again. Only this time towards the path of their God, the God of Israel. It is these women who will have to stand up against the other woman, the Great Whore.

Women Misunderstood

Today in North America there are more black women that go to church than are on welfare. This is suppose to be read in a positive way. At least there is one area where nothing bad can be said about these Forgotten Israelites. WRONG! There should have been no comparison in the first place, and there is nothing positive about this statement anyway. Attending the Christian church is the root of all of the problems black people face today.

O ye daughters of Israel, you are entering into the twenty first century still worshipping false gods and are so proud of it. IF YOU BELIEVE IN GOD WITH ALL YOUR HEART AND SOUL AND BELIEVE IN HIS WORD AND THE LAWS OF THE PROPHETS AND THE JUDGMENT WRITTEN IN THE HOLY BOOK OF GOD (THE HOLY BIBLE), THEN TELL ME WHAT DO YOU DO AS A CHRISTIAN THAT IS WRITTEN IN THE BIBLE, TELL ME WHAT YOU WOULD NOT DO, BECAUSE IT IS WRONG ACCORDING TO HIS WORD? Thank you.

You would find that both answers would be zero because Christians do not follow any instructions written in the Holy Bible, yet it is their official book of spiritual learning.

If you look carefully you'll find that John 3:16 is always used. The Old Testament, according to Christians, is outdated. There are no more laws to follow now, because Jesus died for our sins and somehow changed them. This is the basic philosophy of Christianity. In a bible of sixty six books, they probably use just the books of Paul and when condensed they use about one page. The preacher would take one verse, and use the entire Sunday morning to talk about it or explain his version or philosophy. Whatever he conceives that verse to mean, the parishioners would leave with the philosophy of the Christian teacher and not that of God. After he has gained their confidence he starts to control every aspect of their life.

When your baby is born it must be baptised by the Christian church. When it is old enough to take a companion, mate, or spouse you must return to the same man of cloth for him to give the O.K. to the marriage. When you are dead your relatives take you back to the same man of cloth for his blessings. His O.K. is needed when you came into the world. His O.K. is needed when you are old enough to make your decisions. His O.K. is needed to legalize the activities of your bedroom. His O.K. is even needed when you are dead. I know you believe that his O.K. is needed even to save your soul after death.

If you should turn your bible from page to page, you would not find any of these instructions. Yet black people, women in particular fill these churches listening to the prophets of false gods, the teachers of doom. Because the women folk attend in such large numbers and believe, they entice their families to believe, not caring whether they will all end up in the pit.

O ye daughters of Israel, why do you take your leadership role so lightly? Look around you, you are in control, you are still leading, but in the wrong direction. You need to remove the shadow from your eyes so you can see clearly. Did you know that more Blackwomen are being hired today by corporations and government agencies than Blackmen? The enemy knows that if the Israelite women are on his side, then the men would be no problem.

Let's examine together how you have been fooled by Christianity and conned by its agents. Because you are out there competing, your sons have become uncircumcised and you cannot see the price being paid for this folly. Women should know, especially Blackwomen, that the education of their children starts from conception. You educate your child from the womb. Therefore today's woman must always be aware that they help to form the characteristics and mould the personality of the unborn child.

A child's personality is moulded from the time he or she is conceived, to approximately three to five years old. After this time, it will almost be impossible to straighten the child's bended ways. Here is an example for you to take a very close look at. I am sure you have not paid much attention to it. Take a young bride that worshipped the man when she became pregnant by him, the baby would have the characteristics of her husband. In most cases the child would look like its daddy. Then if you watch the relationship between the spouses deteriorate, the children that will follow would take on their own characteristics and looks. If the mother has a strong will or a domineering personality, then the child will take some of the characteristics of the mother. That is why most first-born resembles their father. Most foster parents with this knowledge, will adopt a baby from birth to five years, and in this way, it would be easier to train the child. Other foster parents without this knowledge, often end up with an older child and more problems. This is one of the ways you can battle the ignorance of your spirituality by education.

The jails are full with bone of your bone and flesh of your flesh. The streets are also full of your sons pan-handling for a meal, doing everything he knows to survive. Sometimes he ends up on the other side of the gun. He cannot have a family, because he is not equipped to maintain that family, so his pride runs away and he runs with it. Another woman takes your place, and this is done all over again. Your daughter does not know anything about raising a family, because you could not teach her, you never had the time. Now she knows nothing of her leadership role. She is out there making more sons for the correctional institutions and more daughters to follow her example of ignorance.

If you understood the laws of your God, as a member of the Forgotten Tribes of Israel you would have taken your rightful place in society. First, you should have looked after your sons, for they would be your protector and your shield. They also would protect the laws and customs handed down by their forefathers. Believe me when a son loves his mother, he would love his wife. What is the first thing you do to your sons as Israelites? You circumcise him according to the law of an Israelite as it is written in your book of laws, the Holy Bible. You circumcise your sons on the eight day with a feast.

CIRCUMCISION & YOUR BABY

Genesis 17:9-14 "And God said unto Abraham, Thou shalt keep my covenant therefore, thou, and thy seed after thee in their generations.
This is my covenant, which ye shall keep, between me and you and thy seed after thee: every man child shall be CIRCUMCISED.
And ye shall CIRCUMCISE the flesh of your foreskin: and it shall be a token of the covenant betwixt me and you.
And he that is eight days old shall be CIRCUMCISED among

you, every man child in your generations, he that is born in the house, or bought with money of any stranger, which is not of thy seed.

He that is born in thy house, and he that is bought with thy money, must needs be circumcised: and my covenant shall be in your flesh for an EVERLASTING COVENANT.

And the UNCIRCUMCISED manchild whose flesh of his foreskin is not circumcised, that should shall be cut off from his people: he hath BROKEN MY COVENANT."

This is the first law of the circumcision. There is no law written in the books of the prophets that state you should baptize your baby. You should follow the instructions and commandments of God and not those of man. You are a chosen of God and you should always remember that it was a Pope who made the law to baptize your babies, to enable him to control your entire life spiritually, from birth to death. It was Pope Innocent VIII who played God in his day by ignoring God's law and creating his own.

The law of circumcision is consistent with God's law. Joshua 5:2-5 "At that time the Lord said unto Joshua, make thee sharp knives and CIRCUMCISE again the children of Israel the second time.

And Joshua made him sharp knives, and circumcised the children of Israel at the hill of the foreskins.

And this is the cause why Joshua did circumcise: All the people that came out of Egypt, that were males, even all the men of war, died in the wilderness by the way after they came out of Egypt.

Now all the people that came out were circumcised: but all the people that were born in the wilderness by the way, as they came forth out of Egypt, them they had not circumcised."

We notice that the children of Israel had to be circumcised to receive anything from God. In the story of Abraham, he had to be circumcised so that he could receive the covenant and the circumcision was part of that covenant. We learned that the children of Israel resided in the wilderness for forty years because they disobeyed God. They had to be circumcised, to receive the land (Israel). Exodus 12:48 "And when a stranger shall sojourn with thee, and will keep the Passover to the Lord, let all his males be circumcised, and then let him come near and keep it: and he shall be as one that is born in the land: for no uncircumcised

94

person shall eat thereof."

In this chapter we learn that to keep the Passover one must be circumcised (Note: not communion, neither baptism), for the uncircumcised could not participate in such a holy commune with God. Jeremiah 4:4 "CIRCUMCISE yourselves to the Lord, and take away the foreskin of your heart, ye men of Judah and inhabitants of Jerusalem: Lest my fury come forth like fire, and burn that none can quench it, because of the evil of your doings."

In this scripture we learn that not only the foreskin should be circumcised, but the heart also.

When your Christian teachers read this, they tell you that you no longer need to be circumcised because God changed the law. What the last scripture really meant is that you should not only circumcise your foreskin and still worship false gods or turn to other customs. When the foreskin is circumcised and you circumcise your heart, meaning to make it pure, to cut off the covering of falsehood and turn back to the God of Israel, you would be welcome back in God's family. For there is no other God in heaven or under, that is mightier than He. If God had stopped circumcision then why were Jesus and John the Baptist circumcised?

Luke 2:21 "And when eight days were accomplished for the CIRCUMCISING of the child, his name was called Jesus, which was so named of the angel before he was conceived in the womb."

Luke 1:54-60 "He hath holpen his servant Israel, in remembrance of his mercy;

As he spake to our fathers, to Abraham, and to his seed FOREVER.

And Mary abode with her about three months, and returned to her own house.

Now Elisabeth's full time came that she should be delivered: and she brought forth a son.

And her neighbours and her cousins heard how the Lord had shewed great mercy upon her; and they rejoiced with her.

And it came to pass, that on the eighth day they came to CIRCUMCISE the child: and they called him Zacharias, after the name of his father.

And his mother answered, Not so; but he shall be called John."

After reading these scriptures we notice that the tradition of Israel still stood strong in the days of Jesus and John the Baptist for both boys were circumcised as Israelites, not baptized as Christians. Please note the role of their mothers. We will further find out that these same Israelites written about in the bible were all called children of the circumcision. It is no coincident that they have been separated from others, because the Almighty God has a reason for everything. All of His chosen were circumcised. So how dare these Christian teachers tell you not to circumcise your sons on the eighth day. How dare they! Acts 7:8 "And he gave them the covenant of circumcision; and so Abraham begat Isaac, and CIRCUMCISED him the eighth day: and Isaac begat Jacob: and Jacob begat the twelve patriarchs."

You, the Forgotten Israelites, children of slavery, are the children of Israel. You are the children of the circumcision. Acts 10:45 "And THEY OF THE CIRCUMCISION which believed were astonished, as many as came with Peter, because that on the Gentiles also was poured out the gift of the Holy Ghost."

Acts 11:1-3 "And the apostles and brethren that were in Judaea heard that the Gentiles had also received the word of God. And when Peter was come up to Jerusalem, THEY THAT WERE OF THE CIRCUMCISION contended with him.
Saying, Thou wentest in to men uncircumcised, and didst eat with them."

We will learn that the Gentiles do not have to be circumcised because they are not of the circumcision, they don't care. That is why their doctrine is against circumcision because they don't have to. Just take a look at the results. They are the ones that are flourishing and the Forgotten Israelites are in the gutter.

Concerning the Gentiles it is written in Acts 15:14-20 "Simeon hath declared how god at the first did visit the Gentiles, to take out of them a people for His name.
And to this agree the words of the prophets; as it is written.
After this I will return, and will build again the tabernacle of David, which is fallen down; and I will build again the ruins thereof, and I will set it up:
That the residue of men might seek after the Lord, and all the Gentiles, upon whom my name is called, saith the Lord, who doeth all these things.
Known unto God are all his works from the beginning of the

96

world.

Wherefore my sentence is, that we trouble not them, which from among the Gentiles are turned to God:

But that we write unto them, that they abstain from pollutions of idols, and from fornication, and from things strangled, and from blood."

Here it is made very clear. Yet God's people would not adhere to the laws of their fathers according to the scriptures. The entire teachings of Israel have fallen down. The tabernacle of David is in ruin, so God has now turned to the Gentiles, but made it quite clear that they are not the children of the circumcision. This would put to shame the Christian myth that God loves everybody. That's why we prove it from the book of Acts which is considered by Christians to be the foundation of their teachings.

The teachings of Paul and the yearning to know more about him is more important to some Christians than Jesus. Yet we find that Paul is being identified with the God of Israel and not those of Christianity. He also speaks of circumcision and the children of the circumcised in verses 23-29.

This again shows the separation of the children of the circumcision from the Gentiles. For God had said that the day cometh when He would punish the circumcised and the uncircumcised because even though they might be circumcised in the foreskin their hearts are not. Jeremiah 9:25-26 "Behold, the days come, saith the Lord, that I will punish all them that are CIRCUMCISED with the UNCIRCUMCISED.

Egypt, and Judah, and Edom, and the children of Ammon, and Moab, and all that are in the utmost corners, that dwell in the wilderness; for all these nations are uncircumcised, and all the house of Israel are uncircumcised in the heart." This does not mean you should not circumcise your sons.

The line is drawn in the laws of God. For Timothy was of mixed race, and Titus was a Greek (Gentile). That is why their cases to be circumcised or not raised eye brows in their day. For the teachers of the New Testament, taught from the Old Testament. Acts 28:23 "And when they had appointed him a day, there came many to him into his lodging; to whom he expounded and testified the kingdom of God, persuading them concerning Jesus, both out of the law of Moses, and out of the prophets, from morning till evening."

This is said about Timothy in <u>Acts 16:1-3</u> "Then came he to Derbe and Lystra; and, behold, a certain disciple was there, named Timotheus, the son of a certain woman, which was a Jewess, and believed; but his father was a Greek;

which was well reported of by the brethren that were at Lystra and Iconium.

Him would Paul have to go forth with him; and took and circumcised him because of the Jews which were in those quarters; for they knew all that his father was a Greek."

Read about Titus in <u>Galations 2:3</u> "But neither **Titus,** who was with me, **being a Greek** was compelled to be circumcised."

If the children of slavery do not believe that they are the children of the circumcision why do they pray and read the bible? They should know that the teachings written in the bible are the teachings of the children of Israel.

This is what Titus said of them and he was a Greek. <u>Titus 1:10</u> "For there are many unruly and vain talkers and deceivers, specially THEY OF THE CIRCUMCISION,"

Even this teacher of the gospel, being Greek classified himself not as a child of the circumcision, but openly admitted that he was a Gentile.

Again the difference, the circumcised and others. So Daughters of Zion, Daughters of Israel, you The Forgotten Daughters. Please circumcise your sons.

MARRIAGE AND YOU

Do you honestly believe that you were meant to stand before a man and repeat a million "I DO'S" or "I WILL'S" while you are being married? Just like the baby being baptised by this man, who takes control of your spiritual life from birth and continues to control it at the height of your maturity. This man stands before you allowing you to repeat after him. In other words without this Christian male standing before you your marriage becomes null and void.

What a shame, what a shame! What Christianity has done to God's chosen people. Without realizing it you are worshipping this man. To take an oath is serious business, especially when you call upon a god. You always swear by a god when you repeat what the man in front of you tells you to say and if you are not calling on the God of Israel, then you are calling on the spirits of the damned. So that spirit is with you from your birth, in your marriage and at your death.

Let's deal with marriage now. Because we do not understand the ways of the spirit, we plunder our bodies with the excuse given to us by our Christian teachers, giving you the freedom to sleep with whom you please, because you believe in your heart that you are not married yet. This is a favourite line used very often in relationships by both men and women.

If you approach your Christian teacher to ask advice, what would be the first thing he would ask? Are you married? If your answer is "No sir, we are living together." His answer would be "You would have to be married first, because you are living in sin."

Again here is your Christian teacher, a mere man playing God. Who gave him the right to judge you? Is it written in the scriptures? Then show me where it says if two people live together it means they're living in sin. Christianity has created a stinking morality law all by themselves and not with the help of God. As usual it is Christian teachers who play God.

God has created woman with a veil in her vagina. With this veil this woman is either called a virgin or maiden. In the scriptures this veil is called maiden. In today's teaching it is called the woman's virginity, but if you notice very carefully there is not much of this around today among the Daughters of The Forgotten Israelites. Why? Because the Christian society had placed less and less importance on this, while placing more and more importance on the church and the long white dress and the flower girls and the man that you stand before. This is almost every young girl's dream to walk down the aisle with the flower girls. Sometimes even the husband is not as important as the parade. This pagan custom has caught on in the hearts of the Daughters of Israel.

It was, and still is considered by Israelites that the breaking of the maiden through male penetration is true marriage. The pagans have removed the veil from where God had placed it and put it on the bride's head-dress. The veil on this head-dress covers her face. Then the man raises that veil on the hat and kisses

99

you on instruction from the Christian teacher, who then pronounces you husband and wife.

Note how this man has taken the place of God. First, he instructs the man to raise the veil of the hat, which is symbolic of raising the skirt of the woman. Then he orders him saying "You may kiss the bride" which is symbolic of the sex act.

God said "Take her to wife." The man says "You are now husband and wife." Knowing the truth about marriage will give you a better understanding of divorce. "I can do it now, but when I get my husband I'll stop."

Now the Daughters of the Forgotten Israelites are given the O.K. to go a whoring with their bodies, because they are not married according to the Christian laws.

Let's try to analyze the meaning of marriage through the scriptures. When does a woman become a wife? We are going to discover what God says.

You'll find the instruction in the first marriage in Genesis 2:23-25. There was no ceremony here, the other person apart from Adam and Eve was God Himself. The second marriage was just two people, Cain and the woman. I wonder who made the woman a wife? Genesis 4:17 "And Cain knew his wife; and she conceived, and bear Enoch; and he builded a city, and called the name of the city, after the name of his son, Enoch."
The scriptures say he knew his wife and she conceived. We are very sure that he just did not say hello when she conceived. He penetrated her and she became his wife, then conceived. In Genesis 38:7-10 "And Er, Judah's first born, was wicked in the sight of the Lord; and the Lord slew him.
And Judah said unto Onan, GO IN UNTO thy brother's wife, and MARRY her and raise up seed to thy brother.
And Onan knew that the seed should not be his, and it came to pass, when he went in unto his brother's wife, that he spilled it on the ground, lest that he should give seed to his brother.
And the thing which he did displeased the Lord; wherefore he slew him also"

You would have noticed that in verse 8 **"Go into her and marry her"** It cannot be simpler than this. This is also seen in the story of Abraham in Genesis 12:18-19 "And Pharaoh called Abram, and said, What is this that thou hast done unto me? Why

100

didst thou not tell me that she was thy wife?
What saidst thou, she is my sister? So I might have taken her to me TO WIFE. Now therefore behold thy wife, take her, and go thy way."

Note here the phrase "to wife" means sex. Genesis 41:45 "And Pharaoh called Joseph's name Zaphnathpaaneah; and he gave him TO WIFE Asenath the daughter of Potipherah priest of On. And Joseph went out over all the land of Egypt."

Deuteronomy 7:1-4 "When the Lord thy God shall bring thee into the land whither thou goest to possess it, and hath cast out many nations before thee, the Hittites, and the Girgashites, and the Amorites, and the Canaanites, and the Perizzites, and the Hivites, and the Jebusites, seven nations greater and mightier than thou;
And when the Lord thy God shall deliver them before thee; thou shalt smite them, and utterly destroy them; thou shalt make no covenant with them, nor shew mercy unto them:
Neither shalt thou make MARRIAGES with them; thy daughter thou shalt not give unto his son, not his daughter shalt thou take unto thy son.
For they will turn away thy son from following me, that they may serve other gods; so will the anger of the Lord be kindled against you, and destroy thee suddenly."

Deuteronomy 25:5 "If brethren dwell together, and one of them die, and have no child, the wife of the dead shall not marry without unto a stranger: her husband's brother shall GO IN UNTO HER, and take her to him TO WIFE, and perform the duty of an HUSBAND'S brother unto her." Following would be an example of the real meaning of husband and wife as you would find in Deuteronomy 21:13 "And she shall put the raiment of her captivity from off her, and shall remain in thine house, and bewail her father and her mother a full month: and after that THOU SHALT GO IN UNTO HER, AND BE HER HUSBAND, AND SHE SHALL BE THY WIFE."

The actions or customs of the husband and wife situation cannot be explained any clearer than in this last verse, which clearly stated that after sex the term husband is being used so is that of wife in the context of marriage.

Deuteronomy 22:25-30 "But if a man find a betrothed damsel in the field, and the man force her, and lie with her: then the man only that lay with her shall die:

101

But unto the damsel thou shalt do nothing; there is in the damsel no sin worthy of death: for as when a man riseth against his neighbour, and slayeth him, even so is this matter:

For he found her in the field, and the betrothed damsel cried, and there was none to save her.

If a man find a damsel that is a VIRGIN, which is not betrothed, and lay hold on her, and lie with her, and they be found;

Then the man that lay with her shall give unto the damsel's father fifty shekels of silver, and she SHALL BE HIS WIFE: because he hath humbled her, he may not put her away all his days.

A man shall not take his father's wife, nor discover his father's skirt."

These scriptures deal with the difference between rape and real marriage. Let us pause here for a while and look deeper into what the white Christians have done to a culture that was unique in the sight of God. Though the children of the circumcision were disobedient to their God, the culture was still intact until they noticed the customs of others and began to copy them, then the wrath came upon them. The Christians seized this opportunity and eventually demolished everything.

Let us read about Jesus and the woman of Samaria. John: 4: 16-18. "Jesus saith unto her, Go, call thy husband, and come hither.

The woman answered and said,I have no husband. Jesus said unto her, thou hast well said, I have no husband:

For thou hast have FIVE HUSBANDS; and he whom thou now hast is not thy husband; in that saidst thou truly".

How do you think your preacher would explain this scripture? Maybe he'll say she had to go before a judge five times, and now she's living in sin. This woman had five husbands that she had sex with, that must have put her away, or she walked out on. She was now living the life of a concubine or a whore, but surely not in sin, according to the white fathers of Christianity. They called the old ways primitive and installed Christianity in your minds and in your hearts. Gradually they changed the circumcised to pagans with a new name. It was considered normal practice for the slave master to take the virginity of a young female slave, sometimes as early as nine or ten years old. What is also sad about this whole situation is that some of these little girls looked

102

forward to the day when their virginity would have been taken by the slave master. It is no wonder that the women folk no longer control that area of their union.

There are five types of women.

1) A virgin 2) A wife 3) A concubine 4) A whore 5) A harlot

1) A virgin: One that has not known a man.One who has never had sex and still carries the veil of the union in her body.

Genesis 24:16 "And the damsel was very fair to look upon, A VIRGIN, neither had any man known her: and she went down to the well, and filled her pitcher, and came up."

Leviticus 21:14 "A widow, or a divorced woman, or profane, or an harlot, these shall he not take: but he shall take a VIRGIN OF HIS OWN PEOPLE TO WIFE."

Deuteronomy 22:13-19 "If any man take a wife, and go in unto her, and hate her,

And give occasions of speech against her, and bring up an evil name upon her, and say, I took this woman, and when I came to her, I found her not a maid:

Then shall the father of the damsel, and her mother, take and bring forth the tokens of the damsel's virginity unto the elders of the city in the gate:

And the damsel's father shall say unto the elders, I gave my daughter unto this man to wife, and he hateth her;

And, lo he hath given occasions of speech against her, saying, I found not thy daughter a maid; and yet these are the tokens of my daughter's virginity. And they shall spread the cloth before the elders of the city.

And the elders of that city shall take that man and chastise him;

And they shall amerce him in an hundred shekels of silver, and give them unto the father of the damsel, because he hath brought

 up an evil name upon a virgin of Israel: and she shall be his wife; he may not put her away all his days."

In the last scripture it describes the custom of the people which was also the custom of the children of slavery. A white sheet would be spread on the bed of the two about to be married and the blood on the sheet from her virginity (fountain), the parents would keep.This would be the case when the wife was chosen by the parents for their son or when the male would bring her for the approval of his parents. There would then be a feast to bind the spirits of the couple. One such feast was attended by

103

Jesus where He performed His first miracle. The couple would then bind the flesh by the breaking of the veil. Sometimes the veil was broken first, then the man would ask his parents to get her for him, meaning to give their blessings; as in the case of Samson in Judges 14:2. For a very good example of virgin, maiden and marriage, you can read about the differences between Leah and Rachel. We would read where Leah gave her maiden to her husband Jacob. She revealed this statement after she had given birth to her son Issachar. Genesis 30:18 "And Leah said, God hath given me my hire, because I have given my maiden to my husband: and she called his name Issachar."

Another fine example would be the story of David and Bathsheba, where Bathsheba is constantly mentioned as Uriah's wife, even after she was with David. This was because she had given her maiden to Uriah the Hittite and still David took her for his wife after he had sex with her (A Hittite was a white skinned man. They once occupied the land we know as Turkey).
II Samuel 11:3.

In the verses that follow you would learn how David arranged the death of Uriah, so he could have his wife. In the verse 26-27 we learn of her husband's death. "And when the wife of Uriah heard that Uriah her husband was dead, she mourned for her husband.
And when the mourning was past, David sent and fetched her to his house, and she BECAME HIS WIFE, and bare him a son.
But the thing that David had done displeased the Lord."

What displeased the Lord was the fact that David wilfully sent Uriah to his death, so that he could make Bathsheba his wife.

In II Samuel 12:10 you will notice where it says you take the wife of Uriah to be thy wife. This simply means to have sex. Let's now read verse 24. "And David comforted Bathsheba HIS WIFE, and went in unto her, and lay with her: and she bare a son, and he called his name Solomon: and the Lord loved him."

Note that no man was standing before Bathsheba and David, it was the act of sex that sealed the bond of marriage. Christianity is the religion of man who places himself wherever there use to be God. That's why there is Santa who knows when you're good or when you're bad. It is because of this man-made religion that the Daughters of the Israelites are so loose. They seem to have no morals anymore. Only the morality of the Christian church that

104

judges over the Forgotten Israelites and is ready to condemn them for being unholy.

2) To wife: means sex. Long after this biblical era, this slang or statement was still being used. Rather than using the word "sex" the word "wife" was used instead. Up to the time of slavery and shortly after, as late as the mid seventies, this phrase was used and in some parts of the world is still being used.

For a wife: This means that when a man and a woman engage in sexual activities, the woman automatically becomes the wife. There are two types of wife.

a) One who submits her virginity or maiden to the man who becomes her husband.

b) A woman who was already a wife, had already lost her virginity, found favour with another man who then entreated her as a wife. He must announce to his family and friends that he has taken her for a wife.

3) A concubine: One who openly sleeps with a man who has never admitted to anyone that he had taken her for a wife. Yet she continues to be a part of his sex life, knowing that he has a wife. This was very common in biblical times. She could easily be put away.

Judges 19:1-2 "And it came to pass in those days, when there was no king in Israel, that there was a certain Levite sojourning on the side of mount Ephraim, who took to him a CONCUBINE out of Bethlehemjudah.

And his CONCUBINE PLAYED THE WHORE against him, and went away from him unto her father's house to Bethlehemjudah, and was there four whole months."

II Samuel 3:7 "And Saul had a CONCUBINE, whose name was Rizpah, the daughter of Aiah: and Ishbosheth said to Abner, Wherefore hast thou gone in unto my father's CONCUBINE?"

As we continue to read the scriptures we are finding the difference between a wife and a concubine. II Samuel 5:13 "And David took him more CONCUBINES and WIVES out of Jerusalem, after he was come from Hebron: and there were yet sons and daughters born to David."

Even Abraham had concubines as we find in Genesis 25:6 "But unto the sons of the concubines, which Abraham had, Abraham gave gifts, and sent them away from Isaac his son, while he yet lived, eastward, unto the east country."

Then we turn to the most famous king of Israel, Solomon and we learn of his love for women. See I Kings 11:3 "And he had seven hundred wives, princesses, and three hundred concubines: and his wives turned away his heart."

We have dealt with three types of women. Let's now deal with the other types.

4) The whore: This woman sleeps with any or every man she can. Some may want to classify a whore with one who takes money for sexual services rendered. This is not true, but there is a possibility that a whore can become a harlot. The woman who takes money for services rendered is called a HARLOT.

Many places in the bible God refers to the whole family of Israel as whores, because the children of Israel always sought after other gods, forsaking their own. This is the mentality of a WHORE - Unsettled, adventurous, unsatisfied.

Leviticus 19:29 "Do not prostitute thy daughter, to cause her to be a WHORE; lest the land fall to whoredom, and the land become full of wickedness."

The children of Israel had also been warned not to take a whore for a wife.

Leviticus 21:7 " They shalt not take a wife that is a WHORE, or profane; neither shall they take a woman put away from her husband; for he is holy unto his God."

Deuteronomy 23:17-18 "THERE SHALL BE NO WHORE OF THE DAUGHTERS OF ISRAEL, nor a sodomite of the sons of Israel.Thou shalt not bring the hire of a WHORE, or the price of a dog, into the house of the Lord thy God for ANY VOW: for even both these are abomination unto the Lord thy God."

Christianity is called the Great Whore. See Revelation 17: verses 1,15,16 and Revelation 19; 2.

We should learn from now on, not to be a whore, then a wife, as the Christians would like the children of God to be by not educating them in truth.

Deuteronomy 31:14-18 "And the Lord said unto Moses, Behold, the day approach that thou must die: call Joshua, and present yourselves in the tabernacle of the congregation, that I may give him a charge. And Moses and Joshua went, and presented themselves in the tabernacle of the congregation. And the Lord appeared in the tabernacle in a pillar of a cloud: and the pillar of the cloud stood over the door of the tabernacle.

106

And the Lord said unto Moses, Behold, thou shalt sleep with the fathers; and this people will rise up and go a WHORING AFTER THE GODS OF THE STRANGERS of the land, whither they go to be among them, and will forsake me, and break my covenant which I have made with them.

Then my anger shall be kindled against them in that day, and I will forsake them, and I will hide my face from them, and they shall be devoured, and many evils and troubles shall befall them; so that they will say in that day, Are not these evils come upon us, because our God is not among us?

And I will surely hide my face in that day for all the evils which they shall have wrought, in that they are turned unto other gods."

In that day could apply to today, for this generation has turned to other gods.

THE UNWED MOTHER

There is no such thing as an unwed mother. The same sexual exercise you went through to conceive, we have learnt is the same exercise which makes you a wife. The white Christians have created all these man-made names so as to place the Forgotten Israelites in a totally different bracket, which would render them unfit, loose, whores, and prostitutes; but eventually their own women fell into the same bracket.

How can a child be born out of wedlock? Remember man made this law to force you into Christianity. If you weren't married according to Christian standards, then you were not married. Automatically you become a whore, wanting to be married so badly, that you sleep around hoping that some man would marry you when he finds you satisfying, not knowing all the time that you were married to the first man. This knowledge would have prevented the Forgotten Israelites from going a whoring both with body and with spirit. The white Christian male has created a social ladder which neither an unwed mother nor her bastard child could climb. According to his standard they were both unfit for society.

107

If this were true then some of the children of Israel were bastards. For Jacob's wife Leah was really married to him as we read in Genesis 30:18. Rachel was also married to him according of the binding of spirits and the sealing of the flesh. But who was Bilhah?

Genesis 30:3 "And she said, Behold, my maid Bilhah, go in unto her; and she shall bear upon my knees, that I may also have children by her." This was Rachel's handmaiden.

Also there is another name apart from wives. Genesis 30:9-10 "When Leah saw that she had left bearing, she took ZILPAH her MAID, and gave her Jacob TO WIFE.
And Zilpah Leah's maid bare Jacob a son."

Are the Christians calling our fathers BASTARDS? There is no bastard born of the **children of Israel**.

Let's try to define the word bastard. Let's be honest about it, so you can relate to your sons and your daughters that the real BASTARDS are the Christians who are the original Gentiles and pagans and heathens, not the children of slavery, not the Forgotten Israelites.

Bastard: 1) An illegitimate child. A child not of Israel.
Non-Israelites were called bastards because they shared not the same father.
2) Any irregular, inferior or counterfeit thing.
3) False, spurious.
4) Resembling, but not typical of the genuine thing.
5) Abnormal, or irregular in size, shape or proportion.

So you can understand when the bible speaks of a bastard it is not saying the same thing as the Christians. The bottom line is A BASTARD IS A NON-ISRAELITE.

Deuteronomy 23:1-3 "He that is wounded in the stones, or hath his privy member cut off, shall not enter into the congregation of the Lord.
A BASTARD shall not enter into the congregation of the Lord; even to his tenth generation shall he not enter into the congregation of the Lord.
An Ammonite or Moabite shall not enter into the congregation of the Lord; even to their tenth generation shall they not enter into the congregation of the Lord for ever:"

108

It is very clear because you have your member cut off or wounded in the stones that you become number five above. The last verse also makes it clear that the nations mentioned are not Israelites. Hebrews 12:7-9 "If ye endure chastening, God dealeth with you as with sons; for what son is he whom the father chasteneth not?

But if ye be without chastisement, whereof all are partakers, then are ye BASTARDS, and **not sons**.

Furthermore we have had fathers of our flesh, which corrected us, and we gave them reverence: shall we not much rather be in subjection unto the Father of spirits, and live?"

Again the scriptures put to shame the Christian lie. You who are Israelites should return to your Father for you are not bastards.

HER WEAKNESS

A woman is unique in every way and that uniqueness can be ruined by the path she chooses in life, especially the women of slavery. The things that appear to be so insignificant in life can very well be the things you should hold on to. We have just dealt with marriage and sex, but in order to understand your strength and weakness we would have to turn back to marriage and sex.

What our mothers, sisters, daughters and aunts do, might not appear to be important for the smooth running of their everyday life. What would be most important might be the subject at hand, MARRIAGE. Did we ever stop to think about this pagan custom, which affects us and can affect us for the rest of our lives?

Let's just say that your wedding day is on the 31st of December. Sister Mildred died on the 28th of December, and her burial is between the 28th and 31st before your wedding. Your Christian priest appears at your wedding ceremony and performs all the "I Do's and I Will's", after officiating at Mildred's funeral. Do you think you would have a perfect marriage? Let's forget for the time being that it is a pagan custom and man- made. We are dealing with the spiritual reality of your entire married life.

First, you should not allow any stranger to stand before you and your mate at this hour of bliss. Secondly, you should not stand in an unclean place to give birth to this aspect of your life; the birth of the unison with your husband. The priest would be unclean for he did not only touch the dead body at the funeral, but took it right to the graveyard in the midst of hollowed ground, the cradle of uncleanliness. He wrestled among the dead. The next disaster is the altar. Every Christian takes their dead to the front of their church, right to the altar. This would make that altar or pulpit unclean. How then can your marriage stay pure and work when the evil of death was at the birth of your marriage?

Numbers 6:6 "All the days that he separateth himself unto the Lord he shall come at no dead body." Numbers 19:11 "He that toucheth the dead body of any man shall be unclean seven days." verse 16 **"And whosoever toucheth one that is slain with a sword in the open fields, or a dead body, or a bone of a man, or a grave, shall be unclean seven days."**
Haggai 2:12-13 "If one bear holy flesh in the skirt of his garment, and with his skirt do touch bread, or pottage, or wine, or oil, or any meat, shall it be holy?
And the priests answered and said, No.
Then said Haggai, If one that is unclean by a dead body touch any of these, shall it be unclean? and the priests answered and said, It shall be unclean."

All these laws stand today but are not recognized by Christianity. It is part of the reason for the continual downfall of the Forgotten Israelites, for God is never among the dead and those who deal with the dead, and things of the dead are considered DEAD even though their eyes are open. Matthew 8:22 "But Jesus said unto him, follow me; and let the dead bury their dead."

How long will the Israelites be kept in mental slavery and in darkness? This bondage is worse than the physical chains. All Israelites should take one day and pray in one accord and ask their Father, the God of Israel, the God of our Fathers, for the gift of the spirit of wisdom and understanding. For it is only through this knowledge can the FORGOTTEN Israelites gain back their respect.

Mark 12:26-27 "And as touching the dead, that they rise: have ye not read in the book of Moses, how in the bush God spake unto him, saying, I am the God of Abraham, and the God of Isaac, and the God of Jacob?

110

He is not the GOD OF THE DEAD, but the GOD OF THE LIVING: ye therefore do greatly err." See also Matthew 22:31-32. Matthew 23:27 "Woe unto you, scribes and Pharisees, hypocrites! for ye are like unto whited sepulchres, which indeed appear beautiful outward, but are within full of dead men's bones, and of all uncleanness."

I hope that this very important phase of your life will be taken very seriously from now on, now that your eyes have been made to see, I hope you would be able to really see.

THE FOUNTAIN

There should be no argument, no debate, no doubt in your minds that at the time of your period you are unclean and you should not go to any altar. You should not touch anything that is holy, you should not teach, and you should not allow any man to have sex with you. This is such a sensitive subject that the Christians who oppose it, white males, generally blow it out of proportion when they read Leviticus 15.

It simply means to use water, which we have in abundance in North America, unlike in the days of our fathers in the generation of Moses, who had lived in the deserts. When you read Leviticus 15 it sounds almost impossible to live up to. So let's approach the scriptures first, then try to analyze what Christians had put away because they could not understand.

Look around you, the trees have a bearing season, your dog and your cat, along with all the other animals have a mating season, except man. It is not that man does not have a mating season, but man chooses to ignore it. The monthly cycle of a woman is not a curse, even though sometimes it is called one, but that is according to the context for which the term is being used. On a more natural term, it is no more than a normal human behaviour, and should not be ignored. It has its reason, and its purpose. Your spiritual survival depends on the knowledge of your creation.

Leviticus 15:19-28 "And if a woman have an issue, and her issue in her flesh be blood, she shall be put apart seven days: and

111

whosoever toucheth her shall be unclean until the even.

And every thing that she lieth upon in her separation shall be unclean: every thing also that she sitteth upon shall be unclean.

And whosoever toucheth her bed shall wash his clothes, and bathe himself in water, and be unclean until the even.

And whosoever toucheth anything that she sat upon shall wash his clothes and bathe himself in water, and be unclean until the even.

And if it be on her bed, or on any thing whereon she sitteth, when he toucheth it, he shall be unclean until the even.

And if any man lie with her at all, and her flowers be upon him, he shall be unclean seven days; and all the bed whereon he lieth shall be unclean.

And if a woman have an issue of her blood many days out of the time of her separation, or if it run beyond the time of her separation; all the days of the issue of her uncleanness shall be as the days of her separation: she shall be unclean.

Every bed whereon she lieth all the days of her issue shall be unto her as the bed of her separation: and whatsoever she sitteth upon shall be unclean, as the uncleanness of her separation.

And whosoever toucheth those things shall be unclean, and shall wash his clothes, and bathe himself in water, and be unclean until the even.

But if she be cleansed of her issue, then she shall number to herself seven days, and after that she shall be clean."

The simplicity of this scripture is right before your eyes. While you are experiencing your period and a man touches you, he would be unclean until he takes a shower with water in the evening of that day. If he has sex with you, he too becomes unclean for seven days. If he has sex with you for example on your third day, he would be made unclean for seven days. His first day would be your third. If you examine these statements properly you would find that if there is no sexual contact between you and your spouse, in seven days you will be clean, by washing or bathing every morning and evening. The same goes for your spouse.

None of these statements are made in a general way, these warnings and instructions are strictly for the children of slavery, (The Forgotten Israelites). Others might not be affected by these warnings, they serve their own god.Black People of the

112

Americas, are the children of the Almighty God, and a father usually punishes his own children, not others. The God of Israel is the creator of the entire world, but father only to Israel.

Anything with blood, as we read in Leviticus 15:1-18 would be unclean. This means that if a man is wounded in battle or bleeds from his nose, or any part of a wound in his body, he too is unclean and if he has sex with a woman and discharge (the seed of copulation) into her, she would be unclean, until they both have a shower in the evening of that day.

If this is not understood properly it would sound like a lot of confusion, but it is not. One is advised in order to be on the safe side, when on your period shower twice a day and do not have sex. Do not perform anything holy, or appear at an altar in any spiritual services, or teach at an altar until after seven days. This brings to mind, whether women should be teachers of the gospel or not? Let us see what the scriptures have to say about that. With the right knowledge and understanding of the gospel.

Let's read I Timothy 2:9-15 "In like manner also, that women adorn themselves in modest apparel, with shamefacedness and sobriety; not with broided hair, or gold, or pearls, or costly array. But (which becometh women professing godliness) with good works.
Let the woman learn in silence with all subjection.
But I suffer not a woman to teach, not to usurp authority over the man, but to be in silence.
For Adam was first formed, then Eve.
And Adam was not deceived, but the woman being deceived was in the transgression.
Notwithstanding she shall be saved in childbearing, if they continue in faith and charity and holiness with sobriety."
I Corinthians 14:34-35 "Let your women keep silence in the churches: for it is not permitted unto them to speak; but they are commanded to be under obedience, as also saith the law.
And if they will learn any thing, let them ask their husbands at home: for it is a shame for women to speak in the church."

This is not saying women cannot teach, but rather ask the permission of her husband. For who can know whether she is unclean or not, apart from herself, except her husband. It is very important for both men and women to be aware.

Some Christians churches argue on both sides of this topic

and none seem to understand. Let me try to teach the Forgotten Israelites. There should be no argument whether you can or cannot. You can teach. There were prophetess among our people, the Israelites. Miriam, Moses' sister was one of them.

Exodus 15:20 "And MIRIAM THE PROPHETESS, the sister of Aaron, took a timbrel in her hand; and all the women went out after her with timbrels and with dances."

Judges 4:4 "And Deborah, A PROPHETESS, the wife of Lapidoth, she judged Israel at that time."

II Kings 22:14 "So Hilkiah the priest, and Ahikam, and Achbor, and Shaphan, and Asahiah, went unto Huldah THE PROPHETESS, the wife of Shallum the son of Tikvah, the son of Harhas, keeper of the wardrobe; (now she dwelt in Jerusalem in the college;) and they communed with her."

Please note that Israelites were not degraded as the Christians would want you to believe, for in the last verse Huldah the prophetess dwelt in Jerusalem and went to college.

Luke 2:36 "And there was one Anna, a PROPHETESS, the daughter of Phanuel, of the tribe of Aser: she was of a great age, and had lived with an husband seven years from her virginity:"

You may then ask, does the bible contradict itself? The answer is no! Please do not forget that the bible is an Israelite book, then how do you expect Christians to understand it? Thank God Almighty I'm an Israelite and know it.

A woman cannot teach if she does not understand the laws. That's why only Israelite women that understand the laws can teach because they would not teach, or place themselves before the altar of God in their uncleanliness. So there is no need to be confused any longer regarding the uncleanliness of the woman for she can really hurt herself spiritually because of ignorance. The bible clearly states relationships between men and women as being equal, but puts forward its instructions when they are clean and when they are unclean. When you are clean the scripture says you can enjoy the equality of that relationship.

Read I Corinthians 11:8-12 "For the man is not of the woman; but the woman of the man.

Neither was the man created for the woman; but the woman for the man.

For this cause ought the woman to have power on her head because of the angels.

Nevertheless neither is the man without the woman, neither the woman without the man, in the Lord.
For as the woman is of the man, even so is the man also by the woman; but all things of God."

This chapter explains the difference in the spiritual things between men and women because in spiritual things it is noted that the woman was made for the man. Therefore her head must be covered in worship unlike the men. With all this knowledge you can see clearly that apart from spiritual things, such as uncleanliness, men and women can both share in the essence of equality.

We read what happened to Jesus because one such woman in her uncleanliness touched Him. Luke 8:43-47 "And a woman having an issue of blood twelve years, which had spent all her living upon physicians, neither could be healed of any.
Came behind him, and touched the border of his garment; and immediately her issue of blood stanched.
And Jesus said, Who touched me? When all denied, Peter and they that were with him said, Master, the multitude throng thee and press thee, and sayest thou, Who touched me?
And Jesus said, Somebody hath touched me: for I PERCEIVE THAT VIRTUE IS GONE OUT OF ME.
And when the woman saw that she was not hid, she came trembling, and falling down before him, she declared unto him before all the people for what cause she had touched him, and how she was healed immediately."

Note that Jesus was in a crowd and everybody was touching Him. Therefore it must be the touching of her unclean hands that affected Jesus spiritually. Now the daughters of the Forgotten Tribes are living in a Christian and ungodly world, and the ways of God may seem difficult, but please take the time to understand and continue to pray for that wisdom.

What we have dealt with so far is the recycling of our problems and spiritual diseases. First, at birth you are being given the evils of the earth through pagan baptism. Then at marriage the forces of evil have been placed in your midst through the man at his dead altar, where you make your vows to the spirit of the dead. Then at the birth of your sons, you leave them uncircumcised and cursed, who then take wives starting the process all over again. Your uncleanliness is ignored and there is no one to teach your generation because you yourselves are ignorant, so the pain increases, the poverty escalates, calamities of the heart and soul are on the rise.

There is no entrance for the saints of God, for all your gates are unclean. It would be a great day when all of God's children will come home.

Isaiah 26:13-21 "O Lord our God, other lords beside thee have had dominion over us: **but by thee only will we make mention of thy name.**

They are dead, they shall not live; they are deceased, they shall not rise: therefore hast thou visited and destroyed them, and made all their memory to perish.

Thou hast increased the nation, O Lord, thou hast increased the nation: thou art glorified: thou hadst removed it far unto all the ends of the earth.

Lord, in trouble have they visited thee, they poured out a prayer when thy chastening was upon them.

Like as a woman with child, that draweth near the time of her delivery, is in pain, and crieth out in her pangs; so have we been in thy sight, O Lord.

We have been with child, we have been in pain, we have as it were brought forth wind; we have not wrought any deliverance in the earth; neither have the inhabitants of the world fallen.

Thy dead men shall live, together with my dead body shall they arise. Awake and sing, ye that dwell in dust: for thy dew is as the dew of herbs, and the earth shall cast out the dead.

Come, my people, enter thou into thy chambers, and shut thy doors about thee: hide thyself as it were for a little moment, until the indignation be overpast.

For, behold, the Lord cometh out of his place to punish the inhabitants of the earth for their iniquity: the earth also shall disclose her blood, and shall no more cover her slain."

TO BE AN ISRAELITE
THE TEXTBOOK

Our book of learning is the King James Version of the Holy Bible. All the different versions of the bible being used today, are a reflection of the ignorance protrayed by its users, not able to understand. They wrap their own understanding like a package in the versions that they use. We find the whole situation very surprising since it was transcribed into English in 1611 by a white king of England, who investigated and researched thoroughly along with his empire's top scholars. Don't you find it rather strange that a white king could not even see the blackness written in all of its text?

It is all a spiritual experience that we take for granted. Why would a white man in the seventeenth century circulate a black historical text book all over the world, even using it for his own spiritual education? Noting that it was in this same century slavery in the New World began. How could a white slave owner tell a slave that that slave looks exactly like the biblical prophets of old, or the description of God's people in <u>Lamentation 4:8</u>?

This would mean 1) that they themselves did not understand, just like Christians today, or they deliberately tried to re-educate you into believing that God was white and white was God. 2)They were made spiritually blind so that during the four hundred years the Forgotten Israelites would never know the truth. That is why in 1953 they became more bold faced in their version to hide this truth. From then on there was version after version. Every denomination fighting hard to suppress the facts, just as Daniel predicted would happen in <u>Daniel 7:25</u> "And he shall speak great words against the most High, and shall wear out the saints of the most High, and think to change times and laws; and they shall be given into his hand until a time and times and the dividing of time."

They are a bit tired now, but nevertheless still trying. The battle is a losing one for Christians and non-Israelites who read the Holy Bible to make their point. They'll find out there is no point to be made on their behalf, for the entire book was written by Israelites for Israelites.

YOUR APPAREL

The long white gowns or skirts that our forefathers wore in their time was meant for those days and for that part of the world. We have been enslaved and brought to a new culture, therefore we do not take steps backward and stumble in judgment and in confusion.

The long white gowns or skirts, are to be worn only in your temple before your altar, while you pray on your face. This is considered a garment of our Fathers to separate us from others before our God. Therefore today it would not be appropriate for us to wear in the streets where unclean people can touch us and hold us. We are not living in the days of Jesus or Abraham. The white gown with our colours are to place us with our fathers spiritually, since it is now unreal for us to be with them physically.

You would not find the spirits of our fathers in an unclean place because they are now considered saints.

Leviticus 5:2-3 "Or if a soul touch any unclean thing, whether it be a carcase of an unclean beast, or a carcass of unclean cattle, or the carcass of unclean creeping things, and if it be hidden from him; he also shall be unclean, and guilty.

Or if he touch the uncleanness of man, whatsoever uncleanness, it be that a man shall be defiled withal, and it be hid from him; when he knoweth of it, then he shall be guilty." How would you know whether the person who touches you on the street is clean or unclean? In the temple the brethren know the laws, they would not be unclean in that temple. This is the reason why we wear the garments that represent our spiritual fathers. In a temple or a place of worship we should separate ourselves from others.

There is another confusing issue about how you wear YOUR HAIR. Frankly speaking, you may wear your hair howsoever you wish, providing you cover your head before the altar if you are a woman. A man does not have to cover his head or allow his hair to grow into heap of wool, to carry out the duties of an Israelite.

To allow one's hair to grow, used to be the statutes of a Nazarite, a protector of the laws of Israel. A Nazarite had to be chosen by the High-Priest, who himself had to be chosen by the council of Israel. Then that person who was chosen to be a Nazarite, had to take various oaths (vows), then there would be symbols of that oath. For example,the symbol of Samson was his hair. It doesn't necessarily mean that all who took the oath of the Nazarite would have long hair. David's son Absalom had long hair, yet he was not a Nazarite, as a matter of fact, this long haired (dread-locks) man wanted to kill God's anointed, his own father. 11 Samuel 14:25-26 "But in all Israel there was none to be so much praised as Absalom for his beauty: from the sole of his foot even to the crown of his head there was no blemish in him.
And when he polled his head. (for it was at every year's end that he polled it: **because the hair was heavy on him.**Therefore he polled it): He weighed the hair of his head at two hundred shekels after the king's weight."

What was important for a Nazarite, was to look over the laws and live by them, like John the Baptist, Samson, and others. John the Baptist did not have dread locks like Samson or Absalom. It is very difficult to be a Nazarite. All Israelites are not automatically a Nazarite, but all Nazarites are Israelites. A Nazarite cannot take wine nor grapes at any time, they must adhere to all Holy Days.

Numbers 6:2-3 "Speak unto the children of Israel, and say unto them. When either man or woman shall separate themselves to vow a vow of a Nazarite, to separate themselves unto the Lord. He shall separate himself from wine and strong drink.And shall drink no vinegar of wine or vinegar of strong drink.Neither shall he drink any liquor of grapes nor eat moist grapes, or dried."
Here we have long hair as a symbol of faith, and a symbol of hate. In the New Testament, it is noted in I Corinthians 11:14. "Doth not even nature itself teach you that, if a man have long hair, it is a shame unto him."

Again it is proven how empty is the long hair without the knowledge of purpose.
Numbers 6:6 "All the days that he separateth himself unto the Lord, he shall come at no dead body." The 9th verse reads, "And if any man die very suddenly by him, and he hath defiled the head of his consecration; then he shall shave his head in the day of his cleansing. On the seventh day shall he shave it."

The ones today who claim that the dread locks are for religious purposes must at some time of their lives attend funerals or funeral homes, or must in some way make contact with the dead, or with people who have made contact with the dead, known or unknown. The questions remains, would they shave their head? The style is so fashinable for today's youth that I doubt it. It is impossible in today's society where everyone is not knowledgeable about spiritual things, for you to be separated.

Do not be confused by those who are confused.

INCENSE

Do not burn incense in an unclean place for the same incense will attract whatever unseen is present. If incense is burnt in a clean environment the result will be far more effective. You never burn incense on the streets among unclean people.

When incense is burnt in an unclean place, the person or persons that are burning the incense must be physically and spiritually clean. The only reason why one would burn incense in an unclean place is to do battle with the unclean spirit, hence your spiritual preparation of cleanliness.

II Corinthians 6:17-18 "Wherefore come out from among them, and be ye separate, saith the Lord, and touch not the unclean thing: and I will receive you.
And I will be a Father unto you and ye shall be my sons and daughters, saith the Lord Almighty."

USE WATER NOT WINE

Do not use wine for any spiritual reason. Do not drink wine before your altar or perform any ceremony that is spiritual with it. It is not written anywhere in the Holy Scriptures that you should do this. Wine is referred to in the scriptures to drink when you are physically sick, for your stomach, or your infirmities, not before your altar.

I Timothy 5:23 "Drink no longer water, but use a little

wine for thy STOMACH'S SAKE and thine often INFIRMITIES."

The only other place in the scriptures that mentions the drinking of wine is in Leviticus. This is where our Fathers drank wine at the feast of their harvest in the land of Israel.

Leviticus 23:9-13 "And the Lord spake unto Moses, saying, Speak unto the children of Israel, and say unto them, When ye be come into the land which I give unto you, and shall REAP THE HARVEST, thereof, then ye shall bring a sheaf of the first-fruits of your harvest unto the priest:

And he shall wave the sheaf before the Lord, to be accepted for you: on the morrow AFTER THE SABBATH the priest shall wave it.

And ye shall offer that day when ye wave the sheaf an he lamb without blemish of the first year for a burnt offering unto the Lord.

And the meat offering thereof shall be two tenth deals of fine flour mingled with oil, an offering made by fire unto the Lord for a sweet saviour: and the drink offering thereof shall be of WINE, the fourth part of an hin."

Please note that the children of Israel used the wine AFTER THE SABBATH. It was never used on God's altar. That is why Jesus made it at a wedding, not in a church. Read John 2:7-9. The power of water is with us in every aspect of our lives.

Let's turn now to the creation of all things and prove that water was the source of all creation. Genesis 1:1-10 "In the beginning God created the heaven and the earth.

And the earth was without form, and void; and darkness was upon the face of the deep. And the Spirit of God moved upon the face of the WATERS.

And God said, Let there be light: and there was light.

And God saw the light, that it was good: and God divided the light from the darkness.

And God called the light Day, and the darkness he called Night. And the evening and the morning were the first day.

And God said, Let there be a firmament in the midst of the WATERS, and let it divide the waters from the WATERS.

And God made the firmament, and divided the WATERS which were under the firmament from the WATERS which were above the firmament: and it was so.

121

And God called the firmament Heaven. And the evening and the morning were the second day.

And God said, Let the WATERS under the heaven be gathered together unto one place, and let the dry land appear: and it was so. And God called the dry land EARTH; and the gathering together of the waters called he SEAS; and God saw that it was good."

Water is original as you just read. Wine is a dangerous, demon worshipping practice.

THE CROSS

Now why would anyone, given the facts of reality, cherish an instrument of death. This unclean instrument which killed your Saviour, the instrument that burns at the hands of your enemies to destroy you and your twin brother, EDOM. For those that burn the cross hate both black people and Edomites (you call Jews).

Have you ever stopped to think about the reality of all this? How can an instrument made by the Romans that killed our fathers be holy? It makes me so mad to see the stupidity of black educators, following in the footsteps of pagans. Some of these educators even label themselves as experts. I challenge anyone to prove to me where it is written in the Holy Bible that the children of Israel, after the death of Jesus the Christ, were told to worship a cross, now that it is holy. Ask the K.K.K. They might have a better answer for you.

When the cross is mentioned in the bible note it is always the CROSS OF CHRIST, the one the Romans used to kill Him. To take up the cross means to TAKE UP THE FIGHT. To continue the work that He came to do. Teach the truth TO THE CHILDREN OF ISRAEL. It is not to get two pieces of wood, nail them together and worship it, or to put it all over your clothes. It is not suppose to be a spiritual burden on your body by imprinting the imaginary sign of death and destruction on yourself or to wear around your neck. How dumb can you be. Would God tell you to worship an instrument that killed His servants?

Galations 5:11 "And I, brethren, if I yet preach circumcision, why do I yet suffer persecution? then is the offence of the cross ceased."

122

What is the offence of the cross? TRUTH. Spiritually it is just as heavy as when He bore it physically. John 19:17 "And he bearing his cross went forth into a place called the place of a skull, which is called in the Hebrew Golgotha:
Where they crucified him, and two other with him, on either side one, and Jesus in the midst."

How can a people continue to worship the symbol that enslaved them, the symbol of Christianity. This instrument that killed their forefathers, that Jesus was nailed upon? This instrument that others burn as a token of their undying love for Christianity, and their committed hatred for the Blackman. How can something with so much blood, that caused so much anguish, be holy?

When the bible speaks of Israelites following others, and worshipping their god of the dead, what do you think it means? Psalms.106:28 "They joined themselves also unto Baal-peor, and ate the sacrifices of the DEAD".

The most tragic thing that a black person can do is to worship this symbol of death. Leave it to the white supremacist groups. They are the symbol of the enemies of God. The cross is the symbol of death. Two of a kind. THE CROSS IS NOT FOR THE FORGOTTEN ISRAELITES.

HOW TO WORSHIP

Do not call any man Father. Matthew 23:9 "And call no man your father upon the earth: for one is your Father, which is in heaven."

Do not call any man Reverend. Psalm 111:9 "He sent redemption unto his people: he hath commanded his covenant for ever: HOLY AND REVEREND IS HIS NAME." God is holy and reverend, not man, unless you see the man in front of you at his pulpit as a god. Then call no man reverend.

Do not kneel, clasp your hands and close your eyes to pray. None of our fathers prayed like that, these are all pagan ways. None such instructions are written in the bible. An Israelite prays with his face to the ground or his hands in the air above his head. Even Jesus prayed like this. Mark 14:35 "And he went forward a little, and fell on the ground, and prayed that, if it were possible, the hour might pass from him."

I Timothy 2:8 "I will therefore that men pray everywhere, **lifting up holy hands**, without wrath and doubting."

Call upon the God of Abraham, the God of Isaac and the God of Jacob, for this is His name forever. Exodus 3:15. "And God said moreover unto Moses, Thus shalt thou say unto the children of Israel, **THE LORD GOD OF OUR FATHERS, THE GOD OF ABRAHAM, THE GOD OF ISAAC, and THE GOD OF JACOB, HATH SENT ME UNTO YOU: THIS IS MY NAME FOR EVER, and THIS IS MY MEMORIAL UNTO ALL GENERATIONS.**"

Call upon the Spirit, "CHRIST" not Jesus. This also is a misconception. Jesus represents body, flesh, man, even the symbol of death. It was Jesus who died, it was the Christ that rose. Jesus was a man, a name given by the spirits. Luke 1:31 "And, behold, thou shalt conceive in the womb, and bring forth a son, and shall call HIS NAME JESUS."

The Spirit is the representation of the father, that Spirit is the Spirit of God, the Christ, the God of our fathers, the God of Abraham, the God of Isaac and the God of Jacob (Israel). From now on know Him as Jesus Christ or Jesus the Christ. For Jesus and Christ are two separate entities rolled into one. If you are spiritually blind you would not be able to see this. Here are some examples. Matthew 16:20 "Then charged he his disciples that they should tell no man that he was JESUS THE CHRIST."

Mark 8:29 "And he saith unto them, But whom say ye that I am? And Peter answereth and saith unto him, THOU ART THE CHRIST."

Luke 22:67 "Art thou the CHRIST? tell us. And he said unto the, If I tell you, ye will not believe:"

John 4:29 "Come, see a man, which told me all things that ever I did: is not this the CHRIST?

Acts 4:26 "The kings of the earth stood up, and the rulers were gathered together against the Lord, and against his CHRIST."

Acts 17:3 "Opening and alleging, that Christ must needs have suffered, and risen again from the dead; and that this Jesus, whom I preach unto you, is CHRIST."

So the next time when you pray, do not call on the name

Jesus alone as most Christians do, remember Jesus is just another name. Pray always to the Spirit, the true and living God. THE CHRIST. Matthew 7:22-23 "Many will say to me in that day, Lord, Lord, have we not prophesied in thy name? And in thy name have cast out devils? And in thy name done many wonderful works?

And then will I profess unto them. I NEVER KNEW YOU: DEPART FROM ME, YOU THAT WORK INIQUITY."

The following is the correct way to communicate with your God. "IN THE NAME OF THE CHRIST, THE GOD OF OUR FATHERS, THE GOD OF ABRAHAM, THE GOD OF ISAAC, AND THE GOD OF JACOB (ISRAEL)."

GOD'S DAY

God's day is not everyday as some of the holier than righteous sinners would like you to believe. Even God Himself worked six days and rested on the Sabbath. How then can man turn this around to say that everyday is man's Sabbath? It is not Sunday either. Sunday was called the Lord's day by the enemies of God, the Romans. Another step for resisting the truth. The law passed in Rome by Constantine on the 7th of March 321 A.D. The bible still maintains Saturday as the Sabbath as the holy day of God. Exodus 20:8 "Remember the SABBATH DAY, to keep it holy."

LUKE 4:16 "And he came to Nazareth, where he had been brought up: and, as his custom was, he went into the synagogue on the SABBATH DAY, and stood up for to read."

Today man is more holy than God, so they make up their own laws as they go along and bury you with them. You must stand up and refuse. Find out if your teacher loves God enough to teach His truth, or love your pocket book, your financial contribution?

THE TRUTH ABOUT
FIRE AND HELL

There is no fire in hell. Hell is cold, wet and miserable. There is no proof anywhere in the Holy Scriptures, that there is fire in

125

hell. What is in the scriptures is that it will be fire that will destroy hell. It is God Himself who has been represented by the element of FIRE that will destroy the coldness in the depths and darkness of HELL. I Corinthians 15: 55 "O death,where is thy sting? O GRAVE, where is thy victory?"

There is no difference between death and hell, like there is no difference between the grave, and the dead. They are all COLD.
Revelation 6:8 "And I looked, and behold a pale horse; and his name that sat on him was DEATH, and HELL followed with him.

There is a difference in spiritual presence. An evil presence would generate a coldness in your body. A natural spiritual presence may generate fear that will cause sweating. There would be an excess amount of heat within your body.

In Toronto's Sunday Sun, March 31,1991, page 20, was the headline. "Vision on Wall, WOMAN SEES FACE OF JESUS." It goes on to say, that this woman claims to have seen the face of Jesus. Now if you don't know what Jesus looked like, how can you recognize him? This is only one aspect, the other is, and I quote. "I was SHIVERING, shaking, I thought I was COLD, so I went to talk to the superintendent," she said. On the way, she ran into another resident who told her it was too hot in the building. She went back to her room, and then saw what she says hadn't been there before.

If this person was educated in the ways of truth, she would have known that the real Jesus wouldn't come through a wet wall, but then again this woman, according to the report is a devout Roman Catholic. What else can you expect?

When your pastor tells you that there is fire in hell, ask him to show you the scripture where it says that. All the burning in hell message that he's talking about would be at the Second Coming at the battle at Armageddon. That's when hell would taste the fury of GOD'S FIRE. There is no fire in hell now. It is highly impossible for fire to be in hell.

Here is a scripture that Christians do not understand. Luke 16:19-25 "There was a certain rich man, which was clothed in purple and fine linen, and fared sumptuously every day:
And there was a certain beggar named Lazarus, which was laid at his gate, full of sore,
And desiring to be fed with the crumbs which fell from the rich man's table: moreover the dogs came and licked his sores.

126

And it came to pass, that the beggar died, and was carried by the angels into Abraham's bosom: the rich man also died, and was buried;

And in hell he lift up his eyes, being in torments, and seeth Abraham afar off, and Lazarus in his bosom,

And he cried and said, Father Abraham, have mercy on me, and send Lazarus, that he may dip the tip of his finger in water, and cool my tongue; for I am tormented in this flame.

But Abraham said, Son, remember that thou in thy lifetime receivedst thy good things, and likewise Lazarus evil things: but now he is comforted, and thou art tormented."

You have just read the story of the rich man and the beggar. A typical example of what can happen after death. On one side comfort, and on the other, torment. Evil does not exist with the element of fire. If evil remains in the dark and cold, there would be no complaint, because evil would be at home, but if on the other hand the coldness of evil had to taste the heat of the burning flames, they would not be compatible. Take the fish for example. It cannot survive on land, and you cannot survive in the water.

Let us analyze the situation thoroughly. There are four elements that sustain this world.

1) The element of Fire (God Himself)
2) The element of Water (First Firmament of Creation)
3) The element of Earth (On which all things dwell; used in the creation of man)
4) The element of Air (God blew into man and gave him life)

I'm sure that you'll agree with me about the last three elements. So I would prove through the scriptures that God does not live in hell and He Himself is fire. It will be fire (GOD HIMSELF) that will destroy hell.

Deut. 4:24 "For the Lord thy God is a CONSUMING FIRE, even a jealous God."

Psalms 18:12-13 "At the brightness that was before him his thick clouds passed, hail stones and COALS OF FIRE.

The Lord also thundered in the heavens, and the Highest gave his voice; hail stones and COALS OF FIRE."

Malachi 3:2 "But who may abide the day of his coming? and who shall stand when he appeareth? for he is like a REFINER'S FIRE, and like fullers' soap:"

II Thessalonians 1:7-8 "And to you who are troubled rest with us, when the Lord Jesus shall be revealed from heaven with his mighty angels,

In FLAMING FIRE taking vengeance on them that know not God, and that obey not the gospel of our Lord Jesus Christ;"

You would also find more proof as you read Revelation. The story of Shadrach, Meshach and Abednego is very popular. These three men of God were thrown into a furnace that was heated seven times hotter than usual, yet the angel of the Lord appeared in the midst of the fire. Read in the third chapter of Daniel from the twelveth verse. So the next time when a teacher tells you a Forgotten Israelite, that you would burn in the fiery pit of hell, you should say "After you Sir."

We are now of the understanding, that the dead is unclean. That touching a dead body is one of the most unclean things for an Israelite. When you have given this some thought, then ask yourself, why are dead bodies COLD? So let the unclean, the dogs, and the enemies of God remain in their coldness.

God is fire and light.

Hell is cold and dark.

Have you ever seen fire coming out of a grave?

THE GRAVE IS A SYMBOL OF HELL

FIRE IS THE SYMBOL OF LIGHT

THE REAL COLOURS OF THE BLACKMAN

The colours of the Blackman are not red, green, yellow and black. These colours have kept him back for ages. There is no spiritual upliftment in these colours that you wear, and shout AFRICA. Have you ever seen the triumph of these colours?

There are no instructions anywhere in the bible that says you were given these colours. I believe that the Blackman is so lost that he is willing to grab any and everything for his identification. The colours of our fathers were stolen and used for the success of others.

Now we use the colours of the damned. Esther 1:5-6

"And when these days were expired, the king made a feast unto all the people that were present in Shushan the palace, both unto great and small, seven days, in the court of the garden of the king's palace;

Where were white, green, and blue, hangings, fastened with cords of fine linen and purple to silver rings and pillars of marble: the beds were of gold and silver, upon a pavement of red, and blue, and white, and black, marble."

The proof of the difference between the oppressor and the oppressed has just been read. King Ahasuerus was ruler over Persia, and Ethiopia, and this is the same area that uses these colours even today. For it was Ethiopia that started today's African colour craze followed by The Gold Coast (Ghana).

These are the colours that enslaved the Israelites. Again showing the difference between the Israelites and the custom of the rest of Africa. If you continue to read when the Israelite won his battle and is rejoicing in his God you would notice his colours in Esther 8:15 "And Mordecai went out from the presence of the king in royal apparel of blue and white, and with a great crown of gold, and with a garment of fine linen and purple: and the city of Shushan rejoiced and was glad."

Please note that nowhere in the scriptures it states that gold is a colour. This too is also a lie. Exodus 28:13-14 "And thou shalt make ouches of gold;

And two chains of pure gold at the ends; of wreathen work shalt thou make them, and fasten the wreathen chains to the ouches."

It was the gold that was sown into the clothing of the colours of Israel. II Samuel 1:24 "Ye daughters of Israel, weep over Saul, who clothed you in scarlet, with other delights, who put on ornaments of GOLD UPON YOUR APPAREL."

The Romans and the British are the ones who stole the colours. Especially the latter who stole the red, white and blue in 1606 after James took the throne in 1603. The colours of the Blackman are RED, WHITE, BLUE, AND PURPLE.

Exodus 26:1 "Moreover thou shalt make the tabernacle with ten curtains OF FINE TWINED LINEN, AND BLUE, AND PURPLE, AND SCARLET: with cherubims of cunning work shalt thou make them."

Use them. They belong to you. Throw away the colours that

129

you were given. They may be the colours of today's Africa, but not the colours of our GREAT MOTHERLAND OF OLD.

YOUR EATING HABITS

Of course you can eat anything that is not poison to your body, but what about things that are poisonous to our spirits.We never give the latter much thought and because of this we end up eating everything that the Gentiles, heathens and pagans eat.

Before we get deeper into this subject, there are somethings that need to be cleared up. There are certain scriptures that Christians quote to provide them with the justification of their pagan habits of eating anything. These are the following scriptures.

Romans 14:1-3 "Him that is weak in the faith receive ye, but not to doubtful disputations.

For one believeth that he may eat all things: another, who is weak, eateth herbs.

Let not him that eateth despise him that eateth not; and let not him which eateth not judge him that eateth; for God hath received him."

This scripture is not for every Tom, Dick and Harry. Let us not forget for one minute that this was a family matter, between Israelites. This is Paul, an Israelite, teaching other Israelites, and not a general statement. This is also a direction by Paul explaining the things you eat and not eat, as you grow in your spirituality, Please note that he mentioned in the first verse "him that is weak in the faith." He is talking about the teachings of the Israelites, and explaining that one should not judge another because of the stage of their spirituality.

Colossians 2:16 "Let no man therefore judge you in meat, or in drink, or in respect of an holy day, or of the new moon, or of the sabbath days:"

All Israelites knew what they were suppose to eat, there was never any argument here, the issue again, deals with one Israelite judging another over the heights and depths of their spirituality. Nowhere is it written, that says you may now eat the things I told your fathers before you not to eat. NOWHERE!

Even though the bible that you read every Sunday tells you what to eat, you still listen to the man who himself doesn't know. If we read Leviticus 11 God has given the children of Israel instructions on their eating habits. He had explained why, and it is because we are special. We are so wrapped up in the doctrine of others, that our own doctrine seems strange. When we ought to be teachers, we remain mere pupils.

Hebrews 5:12. "For when for the time ye ought to be teachers, ye have need that one teach you again which be the first principles of the oracles of God: and are become such as have need of milk, and not of strong meat."

Again it is clear, when we read the last scripture, that it is impossible to give a babe spiritual responsibility. When one is strong in the spirit, he can eat meat (not cursed meat), meaning that he was chosen to do the will of the spirit in truth, and no longer considered a babe.

If we were doing the will of our Father, we would have maintained our role as teachers and leaders, instead of followers. Deuteronomy 14:1-3 "Ye are the children of the Lord your God: ye shall not cut yourselves, nor make any baldness between your eyes for the dead.

For thou art an holy people unto the Lord thy God, and the Lord hath chosen thee to be a peculiar people unto himself, above all the nations that are upon the earth."

If you read further you will find that the instructions are specific, yet we listen to the shallow excuses of pagans who say that Jesus stopped all of this when He came. Again there is no evidence to support this lie. The liars would read Acts 10 to support their claim, but all Acts 10 is telling you is that Peter, being an Israelite, never ate anything that is common, no crawling things, or anything unclean.Then he had a dream telling him to eat such things, because God had made them clean. When this dream is interpreted the unclean and creeping things represented the Roman soldier Cornelius who had faith and believed in this Blackman, Jesus the Christ, the God of Israel. So God had cleansed him because of his faith and made him clean.

This chapter is not talking about pork and ham, snails, lobsters, or any of those things. This chapter is talking about a man, a Roman believer. Verse 19-20 "While Peter thought on the vision, the Spirit said unto him, Behold, three men seek thee.

131

Arise therefore, and get thee down, and go with them, doubting nothing: for I have sent them." That should explain it.

The same reason you cannot dwell in an unclean place to serve God, is that very reason you cannot be unclean for His saints to dwell with you. The same way a temple should be clean for the Spirit of God is the very same way your body should be clean for the visitation of His Spirit.

The things listed in the chapters that you have read gives you the opportunity to choose between physical appetite and spiritual needs. Your body is also a temple of the Lord. II Corinthians 5:16 "And what agreement hath the **temple** of the living God; as God hath said, I will be their God, and they shall be my people."

Why then feed it with uncleanliness like pork for instance. Physically its not good for you. Ask your doctor about the amount of cholesterol it carries with it. Spiritually it is dangerous. All unclean spirits are always being dispatched in the swine, that make it a carrier of evil, demons, etc. A scavenger of spiritual death.

Matthew 8:31 "So the devils besought him, saying , If thou cast us out, suffer us to go away into the HERD OF SWINE." Also read Mark 5:12

Isaiah 65:4 "Which remain among the graves, and lodge in the monuments, which eat SWINE'S FLESH, AND BROTH OF ABOMINABLE THINGS is in their vessels; "

And you eat this thing, this vessel of demons? You are a holy people unto God. Therefore refrain from all uncleanliness.

Remember ninety nine percent of messages, advice and instructions in the Holy Bible are given from God to His people, the Israelites. From the prophets to the Israelites. From Israelites to Israelites. Maybe, just maybe, in the books of Paul, one percent to chosen Gentiles, but the scriptures were never used in general terms as Christians would like the world to believe. No statement is directed to the entire world.

BEFORE YOU GO LET ME LEAVE THIS WITH YOU. All black people in the Americas should get out of all the different denominations and be one people, with one purpose, one love and serve the God of their Fathers; The God of Abraham, The God of Isaac and The God of Jacob (Israel).

A Revolution is needed among the BLACK PEOPLE OF THE AMERICAS,THE FORGOTTEN ISRAELITES. Not a revolution of violence against other peoples of the earth. Neither against each other, we have killed enough of our own people, it is time we all return to our own God, and leave the other religions to the ignorant.

Our role is to teach, and teaching we should do, but we can only do so if we attain knowledge, wisdom, and understanding. We must learn to live together in peace and prosperity with honour and pride. Lead! So that others can follow in the path of wisdom and the path of light. Stand up to be counted as great Israelites. Can you imagine in your mind what a wonderful world it would be?

For a start all pregnant women should start the education of the next generation by teaching their unborn children. Read intelligent books. Take part if possible in intelligent debates. Think always in a positive way and talk to your babies. Prepare them to take up the leadership role. Teach them how to be an Israelite. Let their role models be our fathers written about in the bible.

On the cover of a very popular Christian magazine, the question was being asked. Has Christianity failed, is Christianity dead? If I am allowed to answer this question, the answer would be an overwhelming YES.

The children of God, are the children of Israel, who are the children of the circumcision, who are the children of slavery, who are the black people of the Americas. Yes, you black sons and daughters you are God's chosen children; THE FORGOTTEN ISRAELITES.

If after reading this book, you find that there is a conversation taking place between you and yourself, if for some reason there is still some measure of doubt traveling too and from your mind. I strongly suggest the following.

FOR YOUR IDENTITY AND AWARENESS **READ.**
PSALMS: 105-106.
FOR ACKNOWLEDGEMENT.
PSALMS: 119.
FOR YOUR TOTAL COMMITMENT.
PSALMS: 19-26.

STAND BEFORE THE MIRROR

Stand before the mirror
Look on the other side
Go - Stand before the mirror
And look deep down inside
If the one that's looking back at you
Is the one that isn't true
When you stand before that mirror
What would you do?
Stand before the mirror
Listen to the voice you hear
Go - Stand before the mirror
don't hold back the tear
If the voice you hear from the other side
Saying to you he'll stay and abide
Then stand before the mirror
Stand tall in your pride
Stand before the mirror
Take a good look at yourself
Look deep into that mirror
At the beam of blindness that covered your eyes
The chains of doom that do hypnotize
When you stand before the mirror
You never hear their cries
So stand before the mirror
Look on the other side
Stand up I say - Look deep down inside
And when the search is over You ask - Who am I?
Then shake the shackles clean off your mind
Take another look again down deep inside
Then your eyes will behold all that is true
That the man in the mirror is really you.

Now that you have read the truth about yourself;
Do not turn away like our fathers have done.
Fall on your face, or raise your hands towards heaven
And repeat

THE PLEDGE OF THE ISRAELITES:

I believe in the God of Abraham, The God of Isaac;
And The God of Jacob.
I believe in The God of Israel
I believe in one God
I believe that Christ was manifest in the flesh
Is one God.
Like the old Israel who painted Lamb's blood
On their door-posts
I believe that Christ is the true Lamb
and His blood has been painted upon me.
I believe that the same God of Israel
will protect me from all evils and sickness
Of this world
And I will do my best to keep The Laws, The Statutes
And The Commandments
I believe that my Massiah died for my sins
I believe that He raised from the dead
And I believe that He will come again to judge
the whole House of Israel
I believe that my God has Created
the Heavens and The Earth
And everything upon it.
I believe in one God Who is Holy and Righteous
I believe that The God of Israel is my Father.
There is only One God.
There is Only One God of Israel
I will give my whole Soul and Body And Spirit
To the One God of Israel
For He is Righteous, and He is My Father
Hear Oh Israel: The Lord Our God is One Lord.
Selah, and Selah Amen

Fifth Ribb Publishing is known only for the publishing of its inspirational works pertaining to The Bible and The Blackman by Shadrock:

1) **The Truth The Lie and The Bible.**
2) **The Forgotten Israelites.**
3) **The Word The Israelites and The Damned.** *And*
4) **The Spirit of Egypt in America.**
(the latter no longer in print)

We have however decided, in this new millennium to look for interesting, but educational materials to presents to our readers. Not only scriptural, but also life experiences, and we have found **#5) "The Spirit, The Passion and The Blood"** an extraordinary piece of work.. It describes the evil that is so resident in man. It points out the amount of knowledge the Blackman and woman possesses to practice evil. The evil side of our spiritual gift is always implemented with much enthusiasm, excitement and vigour. It is a pity that the positive side is rarely seen and practiced.
After reading this biographical novel, we wish that you will continue in your support of Fifth Ribb Publishing Books by ordering any or all of the above:

NAME_____

ADDRESS:_____

_____

_____

PHONE:_____

Send me _____Copies of #1_____#2_____#3_____#5
I enclosed $13.95 money order for the first three books and
   $15.95 for #5
Send all Orders to.   **FIFTH RIBB PUBLISHING LTD.**
                      P.O. BOX 287 STATION E TORONTO
                      ONTARIO CANADA M6H-4E2.